55 STRONG

INSIDE THE WEST VIRGINIA TEACHERS' STRIKE

55 STRONG

INSIDE THE WEST VIRGINIA TEACHERS' STRIKE

Edited by Elizabeth Catte, Emily Hilliard,
and Jessica Salfia

Belt Publishing

Ten percent of proceeds from the sale of this book will be donated to a DonorsChoose West Virginia teacher project. West Virginia public school teachers may request a free copy from Belt Publishing.

Printed in the United States of America

First edition 2018

ISBN: 978-1-948742-26-9

Belt Publishing
2306 West 17th Street, Suite 4
Cleveland, Ohio 44113
www.beltpublishing.com

Book design by Meredith Pangrace

Cover by David Wilson

All photos by Emily Hilliard unless otherwise indicated.

Jessica Salfia

Spring Mills High School, Berkeley County

NTROD

I n 1990 I was nine years old, and my mom, a single parent, was a day-to-day substitute teacher in Barbour County, West Virginia. We lived in a trailer at the edge of my Grandpa's farm that was already well past its prime—a tin box that was hot in the summer and cold in the winter, but also where some of the happiest memories of my life take place. However, this time was one of my mom's hardest. She had to feed us and provide for us alone, but she made sure that while she was working day to day to get us from paycheck to paycheck, we thrived. I don't ever remember wanting anything really. She took jobs selling tickets at Friday night football games, worked summers at the City Pool concession stand. She always made it work.

Then, West Virginia teachers went on strike.

Now my mother not only had no health insurance, but no income. I'm not going to lie, we struggled. But it's not the struggle or the contention I remember with crystal clarity—it's the intense pride I remember seeing on my mom's face when we'd drive past the picketing teachers outside Philip Barbour High and she'd blast her horn in solidarity. It's the sign that said "Retired Teacher Vehicle" that my Papaw taped to the side of his rusted out, wooden flatbed,

UCTION

farm use truck that he would drive back and forth in front of the picket lines. When I think about my memories of the 1990 strike, it's the strength and awe I remember, and that I still see in every teacher's face who still say of those days, "We held out until they gave us what we deserved."

And what they deserved was significant—a pay raise that moved West Virginia teachers from 49th in the nation to 31st— faculty senates which allowed teachers to impact school policy, and the training and services needed to improve the quality of education across the state.

Nearly three decades later, I'm a proud West Virginia teacher myself, and the improved working conditions hard won in 1990 have eroded. By the fall of 2016 West Virginia teacher pay was once again well below the national average, and impending changes to the Public Employee Insurance Agency were creating skyrocketing premiums and deductibles, exacerbating the economic strain most teachers were already feeling. After doing the math, many teachers discovered that based on salary and family income the PEIA changes would actually result in a loss of pay.

A pay cut. It was unfathomable.

West Virginia teachers have consistently not been given enough, and have been told to make it work. But make it work we do. We spend our Saturdays organizing fundraisers. We take second jobs at Walmart, waiting tables, doing yard work, selling Mary Kay, all to ensure we can continue making miracles happen in classrooms across this state.

Resources aside, every day in my classroom I have to be the best version of myself. My students and their parents expect me to be engaging, prepared, rested, excited, happy, and an expert in my field. Think about the most important presentation you have ever given—the presentation you prepared weeks for, the presentation that your job depended on.

I do that six times a day, five days a week.

My administrators expect instruction to occur bell to bell. Our school and my performance are evaluated by my students' performance on a test I don't get to see. I have to prepare students for college, for jobs, for scholarships. I teach them to write literary analysis and résumés. To be empathetic, critical, smart, fair, and professional.

My principals and my community expect me to guide my students to success. And now, in this day and age, I must prepare my students for the potential threat of an active shooter. A threat my own mother faced down in her classroom in 2015 when a fourteen-year-old freshmen took her and her class hostage for over an hour. Thankfully that day ended without tragedy. And my hero mother? She was back in her room teaching the next day. This has become our normal. We are expected to take a bullet for the students in our classroom while preparing them to be the future leaders of West Virginia. But we won't be able to afford the medical bills if we survive. And instead of addressing the real crisis, there are lawmakers ready to arm teachers with firearms, but not pay them a living wage.

This is the expectation for teachers. Do more with less. Be exceptional. Be a leader. Make sacrifices.

And like my mother, her sister, her brother, and her father—all teachers—I have diligently tried to exceed these expectations.

In 2015 I received an Arch Coal Teacher Achievement Award, in 2016 I was named Berkeley County Teacher of the Year, and in 2018 won the Stephen L. Fisher Teaching Excellence award from the Appalachian Studies Association. I teach Advanced Placement Language and Composition and creative writing classes, advise the Spring Mills High Diversity Club, advise the school's literary and art magazine, coordinate our homecoming parade, and serve on our school's Curriculum and Instruction Team, the Berkeley County Diversity Council, and the Berkeley County Schools Teacher Advisory Committee. I have also coached track and volleyball, and am married to an educator and coach. It is safe to say I have devoted my life to service and to public education in West Virginia.

I am also the mother of three incredible children, but I have treated the hundreds of kids who have passed through my classroom like they were my own. I have fed and clothed my students. I have sat at my kitchen table with my checkbook trying to decide which bills to pay so I can still afford supplies for my classroom. I have spent my Saturdays chaperoning trips to college fairs and organizing fundraisers to support my students' projects and learning opportunities. I have written hundreds of letters of recommendation for scholarships, colleges, and jobs. I have attended my students' weddings and baby showers. I have held their grieving mothers and spoken at some of their funerals. I have wiped their tears, held their hands, and shared their joy.

And like so many other teachers, I do these things not because it's expected, but because it's what my students deserve, what West Virginia deserves. I believe in public education, and I believe that the most valuable resource we have in this state is our young people. West Virginia is filled with thousands of educators like me who know that that the path forward for our state is strong schools and great teaching. Educators who believe in what they do and who believe in West Virginia.

JESSICA SALFIA

But constantly fighting to "make it enough" for our students, and managing our own shrinking household budgets is exhausting. Even before the walkout on February 22, some of my colleagues were readying their résumés for neighboring Maryland and Virginia, where West Virginia teachers can add $20,000 to $30,000 to their annual salaries. The status quo has already taken its toll: West Virginia schools have more than 700 full-time vacancies, and 38 percent of the state's math classrooms have an uncertified teacher.

I live in a place where I could drive twenty minutes to Maryland or Virginia and nearly double my pay. And I would be lying if the temptation of higher pay so close hadn't given me pause once or twice. But I haven't left because I still believe in West Virginia, because I still believe that West Virginia's children deserve public educators who are smart and qualified and good at what they do. I believe our students need teachers like me and all the other incredible teachers across this state who don't just go to work—but who go to their schools to change the lives of our young people because *we believe in them.*

Believing in West Virginia is why on February 22, 2017 nearly 20,000 West Virginia teachers, bus drivers, and service personnel walked away from the jobs they love, asking for a 5 percent pay raise and the restoration of proper health benefits.

This work stoppage lasted thirteen emotionally charged and exhausting days, and what we didn't know when we walked out of our classrooms on February 22 was that West Virginia would serve as a catalyst for an educational revolution across the United States. Even as I write this my college roommate in North Carolina is messaging me to ask my advice about her protest sign as teachers in her district prepare to rally for respect in Raleigh, North Carolina.

I knew from the beginning of this movement our success would hinge on our ability to elevate teachers' voices, to tell our stories. Author Chimamanda Adichie says in her TED Talk the *Danger of the Single Story,* "Stories matter. Stories have been used to

10

dispossess and to malign. But stories can also be used to empower, and to humanize." The maligning began early in the movement. In our local paper, a member of the West Virginia House of Delegates from Berkeley County wrote an op-ed that said "teachers were threatening to strike against our students." I read that and knew to win this fight we had to use our stories to empower and humanize the brilliant educators fighting for public education across the state. Many lawmakers didn't and still don't understand the miracles teachers work every day or the power our classrooms have to make a real difference in West Virginia because most teachers do the great work they do humbly.

I set out to change the narrative about the West Virginia educator. Even before the work stoppage officially began I wrote op-eds and gave interviews. I called legislators' offices and spoke at length to whoever would take my call about the work I do and my passion for public education. But many of those calls went unanswered, and my voicemails and emails went unreturned or were dismissed. So during the first days of the work stoppage, I took my voice to Charleston.

I had an extraordinary ally in the capitol during this time. My uncle, Delegate Danny Wagner from Barbour County, had been a history teacher for thirty-four years, and had been serving in the West Virginia House of Delegates since his retirement in from teaching in 2014. He was a local leader during the 1990 teacher strike in Barbour County; he stood on picket lines that blocked entrances to schools and he used his body to turn busses away to keep school closed during this strike. I listened to his 1990 strike stories like folk hero tales of old. And it didn't matter that Danny is a Republican, and I am a Democrat. The unity of West Virginia teachers during this movement transcended partisan politics. And in West Virginia you always fight for your family.

When I arrived at the capitol on the first day of the work stoppage, Danny swept me in to his office and began listing off the delegates I should talk to, the ones he thought needed to hear from a passionate, smart teacher. He introduced me from the House floor, ushered me through closed doors, and got me face time with folks who he thought could make a difference. Because of him, I was able to have an hour and a half sit-down with the chair of the House Education Committee, Delegate Paul Espinosa, who despite our differing politics I found to be kind, smart, and reasonable. He was eager to hear my concerns and my story, and desperately wanted to work with teachers to find the best way forward for West Virginia education. Delegate Espinosa and I found a common ground and a mutual respect that I believe played a significant role later when he was chosen as one of the House members of the Conference Committee who would go on to make the final decisions on the pay raise bill. I'd like to think that our lengthy, thoughtful conversation during the first day of the work stoppage played a role in his later support of passing the pay raise.

These days at the capitol were exhausting, but eye-opening. I also learned that unlike Delegate Espinosa many of his colleagues in the West Virginia House and Senate have little regard or respect for public educators. Some seemed genuinely shocked to find that I was smart and articulate, and that I actually cared deeply about my job. I was dismissed, laughed at, and avoided all together. I have to wonder though if this had as much to do with my profession as it did my gender. The majority of teachers in America are women, and women were at the forefront of this movement. There was a clear gender divide between the red-clad folks chanting in the halls and the suit-clad folks sitting in the chambers making decisions about schools they had never seen and students they didn't know. I believe that some of the stubbornness of the West Virginia Senate was because there were several men in those offices who didn't like being told what they should be doing by a bunch of women. I thought about this when a few Senators refused to talk to me. I was actually turned away from a local Senator's office—he wouldn't even see me. When I told his secretary my name and who I was her reply was, "No, he won't be seeing *you*." And I will never forget the way Senate Majority Leader Mitch Carmichael strolled out of the Senate chamber to look down on the chanting teachers waiting in the chamber hall and sneer, his lip actually curling in disgust.

When it was time for me to return home and join my colleagues on the picket line, I used my voice in other ways. I spoke to any reporter who called. I gave interviews, wrote op-eds and essays. I talked about love and about pain. About the incredible joy and sorrow that comes with being a teacher. I wrapped myself in the mantle of fifteen years of service to this state as a public educator and I stood with my sign in the rain and in the snow. I smiled and waved to passing cars even as one man in a truck pulled up, took a long drink of water, and spit it at the feet our assembled picket line. I smiled and waved when another man pulled up to our line, rolled down his window, and yelled, "Get the fuck back to work." I smiled and waved (even though I wanted to scream back) because I wanted the public to know this movement was and is about respect, about quality of life, about love. We were standing outside our schools because we love our students; because we love our schools; because we love West Virginia. No teacher—hell, no person at all—should have to choose between the job they love and a living wage. Teachers, cooks, bus drivers, aides, police officers, prison guards, DHHR workers: we all deserve adequate, competitive pay, but most of all we deserve to be able to live and work in the place we love. We deserve respect.

It soon became clear that the majority of the public does not share the opinion of a few West Virginia Senators, and were (and are) ready to give teachers the pay and respect they deserve. Daily on the picket line we received support and love from our community in the form of homemade soup, sandwiches, and hot coffee. Support came from everywhere.

One cold day on the line, a man came walking up the side of the road toward us. His hair was a bit long and he had a scruffy beard. He was wearing work jeans, boots, and a button-down striped shirt, and he was carrying a piece of brown cardboard with something scrawled across it in black marker. I couldn't read it because he was too far away. I stiffened, and I could feel everyone around me get nervous. Was this a counter protester? We had been shouted at a few times by men who looked an awful lot like this fella. He finally got close enough for us to make out his sign.

Teamsters Local 29 Showing our Support and Solidarity for WV Teachers

My eyes welled up with tears and a hard lump formed in my throat. I watched the man travel down our ranks and shake every single person's hand on our picket line. When he got to me, I couldn't help it, hot tears oozed down both sides of my face.

"Thank you so much for being here today" I said as I shook his hand. His hand was callused and strong. It felt like my Papaw's hand.

Photo: Jessica Salfia

"Thank you. Y'all are doing it for the rest of us, and we are so grateful," he answered, his own eyes misting up.

He stayed long enough to shake every person's hand on the picket line, posed for some pictures, and then he left. I found out later he went to almost every school in Berkeley County and did the same thing.

These are the moments that kept us going, kept us united. And every time I heard a horn blast in solidarity, I thought about my mom laying on her horn and my nine-year-old self in the front seat of our old yellow car watching the picketers outside Philip Barbour High School whoop and wave their signs. And I whooped and waved mine, and I'm sure my proud face was the mirror image of my mom's.

West Virginia Public Employees won this fight because we stayed unified, but also because we occupied the West Virginia capitol and forced our legislators and the public to hear our stories. We refused to stay silent. Just like the teachers of 1990 we demanded that the world know what we're worth and we deserve.

Our movement ignited a fire across the country. Our stories of unity and strength have inspired the teachers of Kentucky, Arizona, Oklahoma, Colorado, and many other states and districts across this nation to stand up and reject the status quo of "not enough." And not just teachers, but unions everywhere have looked to West Virginia as the example of what can be accomplished through unity and the power of a collective voice.

In 2015 author Nikki Giovanni spoke to my students in the auditorium of Martinsburg High School and said, "Every person from West Virginia should be proud to be from West Virginia. Your state exists because you rejected slavery. Because you chose freedom. It is up to Appalachia to show the rest of the world how to be." This book is filled with essays, interviews, and photos that tell the complete story of West Virginia's teachers doing just that— stories of brave teachers who chose to stand up for education— what they believe in. Who chose love and freedom in order to show our students, this state, and this nation how to be. ✖

The transcripts interspersed throughout the book are vox populi "woman on the street" interviews conducted by Emily Hilliard during the strike rallies held at the West Virginia capitol on February 26 and 27 and March 1, 2, and 5, 2018. [Names have been changed unless permission was granted.]

UMWA MEMBER, LOCAL 8843, KANAWHA COUNTY

I'm here because I believe in what the teachers want. I think that legislators have showed all disrespect to workers, and it's just not...the teachers now, it's become more dominant with disrespect to workers, and they're extremely pro business--there's nothing wrong with being business. Our whole leadership of our state, even on the national level, has forgotten about workers. And even on the national level. And labor only asks for a piece of the pie--they're not asking for the whole pie! And you think about the teachers--the money they spend for their education, the things they do on their own, for our children. And then they want to cut their healthcare? Well I know now they got it froze, but they want to go by their annual income of the whole family. And then you think about the money that they make, and then all the schooling the have to go through? That's not right.

I am a teacher of twenty-five years and I am here not just for myself but to support all teachers and state employees. Also my own children-- I have a daughter that's in education that's about to graduate and I know this is gonna determine her future, and my son is a type 1 diabetic and we are already eaten up with costs for his supplies and things, so we need a big change with our insurance.

"We are the ones we've been waiting for."

—June Jordan

Jay O'Neal
Stonewall Jackson Middle School, Kanawha County

September 2016: the first payday of the new school year had arrived. I eagerly opened my online bank account to see how much my yearly step increase would raise my paycheck for the upcoming school year. When I clicked on the account and saw my paycheck, I thought there must have been a mistake. It was no mistake; my step increase was more than eaten up by the new health insurance premiums in the PEIA (Public Employees Insurance Agency) health insurance bracket it had bumped me into. Forget about keeping up with inflation, I would bring home $450 dollars less my second year of teaching in West Virginia than my first.

My wife and I moved to West Virginia in the summer of 2015. I had taught in other states, and had anticipated that moving here meant taking a pay cut, but my wife and I felt that her job, being closer to family, and West Virginia's natural beauty would make up for the lower pay. What we didn't anticipate was a decreasing household income each year.

My coworkers and other teachers in my union shared in my shock and frustration. A few mentioned striking, but that seemed extreme. True, West Virginia had had an eleven-day teachers' strike in 1990 that brought about significant changes to teachers' salaries, benefits, and autonomy, but striking is illegal in West Virginia, and organizing a strike would surely be a years-long process.

November 2016: I attended public hearings discussing the changes (i.e. cuts) to PEIA. I hadn't planned on speaking, but when I went to pick up a normally $8 prescription that ended up costing $80, I changed my mind. Along with many others, I told the PEIA finance board that the steady cost increases were making it difficult for public employees to live and work in West Virginia. Many people shared personal stories of financial hardship and how the proposed changes would devastate them. The changes went into effect anyway.

February 2017: the legislative session began and bills to end seniority, start charter schools, and establish paycheck "protection" were introduced. Nothing was done to help fix PEIA or raise teachers' salaries. Along with many others, I emailed, called, and even went to the capitol to meet with legislators. Nothing changed.

I began to research the state's budget. I found out that in 2006, legislation was passed that eventually lowered the business franchise tax to zero and cut the corporate net income tax from 9 to 6.5 percent. Allegedly, this was to attract businesses to West Virginia and grow the economy, but the state now had fewer jobs and was collecting $180 million less per year than before the tax cuts went into place. The money to raise salaries and fix PEIA was clearly flowing out to corporate shareholders' pockets instead of flowing into the state's accounts.

May 2017: Members of both teachers' unions (WVEA and AFT-WV) discussed, vented, and eventually realized that two of the biggest barriers to change were our legislature playing our unions against one another, and our unions spending time and resources trying to out-recruit each other. This realization spurred me to create a Facebook group called "West Virginia Teachers UNITED," hoping that it would be a space where teachers could work across unions to make our legislature listen. I added teachers from across the state who I knew were interested in making change and asked them to add others.

November 2017: The annual PEIA hearings. This year, my group of colleagues had a plan. Realizing that people who showed up to PEIA hearings were public employees who wanted the same changes we wanted, Emily Comer and I took clipboards to the Charleston hearing and gathered contact information in order to connect people to the Facebook group, which we had re-named "West Virginia Public Employees UNITED." We shared things that were happening and encouraged people to get involved. For instance, Emily livestreamed her rude reception at a committee meeting at the capitol and it went "viral" in the group.

January 2018: Our Facebook group had grown to 1,200 members, who were largely using the group as a forum to discuss PEIA changes. Many public employees had previously been unaware of what was happening to PEIA, but were furious when they found out. When one member asked, "Just curious if there are any talks of striking?" the group saw a large uptick in activity.

At the opening of legislative session, a small group of us brought a banner reading "Public Employee Healthcare, Not Corporate Welfare: Fund PEIA" to the governor's state-of the-state address. I was nervous; there were only four of us there, and I didn't know if this was allowed or if we might get arrested. But we held the banner and shared our video of it to the group. At this point, Emily and I couldn't keep up with all the requests to join the group and recruited more moderators.

On Martin Luther King Jr. Day, WVEA held a rally for education at the capitol. At the rally, we were thrilled—and the legislators present seemed surprised—that the word "strike" was mentioned by union leadership. However, after the rally, teachers and public employees met with legislators, and many came away frustrated. They shared their experiences on the Facebook group. As more people shared their feelings, others felt emboldened to do the same, and anger was building.

February 2018: Our group had grown to over 21,000 members. Four counties (Mingo, McDowell, Wyoming, and Logan) voted to do a one-day walkout. I got chills as I watched them rally in the capitol rotunda on Facebook livestream during planning period. I knew their brave act would spur others on. Two weeks later, seven counties walked out, and, the following Saturday, 10,000 people rallied on the capitol steps, chanting "enough is enough!" in the pouring rain. At that rally, our state unions called for an initial statewide two-day walkout the following week. That walkout ended up lasting thirteen days, resulting in a 5 percent raise for all employees, a "freeze" on changes to PEIA, a task force appointed to fix PEIA, and the elimination of bills that would have further hurt education in West Virginia (charter schools, ending seniority, etc.). United, public employees had forced their legislature to listen. ✖

IN OUR "NECK OF THE WOODS"
WE KNOW HOW TO STAND
WITH COURAGE BECAUSE WE
HAVE WATCHED OUR PARENTS,
GRANDPARENTS, AND
GREAT-GRANDPARENTS STAND
ON PICKET LINES.
THE WILLINGNESS TO STAND
IS A PART OF OUR DNA;
IT IS IN OUR VERY BLOOD.

—Katie Endicott

Katie Endicott
Mingo Central Comprehensive High School, Mingo County

In Mingo County, we are known for our dedication to Jesus, allegiance to coal, and strong familial bonds. We are a passionate people who take pride in our heritage and history. We are home to Matewan, the town that helped coin the nickname "Bloody Mingo" and inspired an Academy Award-nominated film on the Matewan Massacre, one of the bloodiest mine war battles in US history. The Battle of Blair Mountain, the largest labor uprising in US history, is also part our heritage and part of every high school curriculum. Southern West Virginians—and Mingo Countians in particular—are no stranger to labor organization and the word *strike*.

In our "neck of the woods" we know how to stand with courage because we have watched our parents, grandparents, and great-grandparents stand on picket lines. The willingness to stand is a part of our DNA; it is in our very blood. Although there's an understanding that striking is illegal, people in the south fear more serious repercussions: disappointing our ancestors. Therefore, when the WV legislature continued their assault on public education and targeted educators' benefits and pay, it was no surprise the people of southern WV started a grassroots movement that not only spread pertinent information but also helped organize union members into a cohesive and powerful group.

When a group of four legislators sponsored a bill that would change public employee insurance benefits from 80/20 coverage to 60/40 coverage, a teacher made a social media post that profiled these four "enemies of education." The post instantly went viral and created outrage and frustration. Quickly, posts like these became commonplace as teachers around the state started to identify and target those in power who were opposing educators. In the south, teachers Justin and Stephanie Endicott created a Facebook Live video in which they explained and explored harmful proposed legislation. Although the video was originally meant for teachers in Mingo County, it spread throughout the south. Teachers started sending messages to Mr. Endicott and one another asking for more information, and schools began holding emergency faculty senate meetings to discuss the information from the video.

Outrage turned to action when Mingo County union leaders called for a county-wide meeting open to members from all three unions: the National Education Association, American Federation of Teachers, and West Virginia Service Personnel. This act of unity surprised and emboldened educators from across the county. When the meeting was publicized, educators from other counties started demanding meetings. Quickly, leaders in over seven counties arranged emergency meetings. Teachers and staff were unifying and mobilizing across the state.

On January 23, approximately 250 Mingo County educators and service personnel crammed into the Care Center in Delbarton. The energy in the room was palpable. There was a mix of frustration over the proposed legislation but excitement at the tremendous turnout. In Mingo County we are all "church folk," and as everyone took their seats you could feel that we were preparing for a spiritual experience. Throughout the nearly three-hour meeting there were four specific moments that shifted the atmosphere and led to the historic decision to come. The first was when state Senator Richard Ojeda stood before the crowd with grit, fire, and passion. His message was very simple: you are worth more. The crowd interrupted his speech numerous times with thunderous applause. Members of the crowd shouted "amen," "yes sir," and "that's right" throughout the passionate speech. As he closed, he looked around the room with purpose in his eyes and said: "Make no mistake about it ladies and gentleman, you have choices to make, and whatever you choose to do, I'll be standing right there beside of you." Again, the crowd roared. It was clear. We had choices. We were going to have to make a decision.

After Senator Ojeda energized the crowd, our regional union representatives, Mr. Brandon Tinney and Mr. Allen Stump, spoke. They provided a comprehensive overview of the upcoming changes to healthcare and salary. Sensing the direction of the crowd, Mr. Tinney and Mr. Stump gently warned us of the consequences of an action such as a blue-flu day. The crowd started laughing and murmuring, "What are they going to do? Fire all of us?" Mr. Stump cleared his throat and spoke with confidence, "Ultimately, we have to do our due diligence and let you know of both the possible risks and rewards. You don't work for us. We work for you. If you choose to do something, we will be standing right there with you. We will fully support you."

While the information about punitive retribution didn't completely stifle the crowd, it had slightly changed the atmosphere—especially amongst the younger educators. Hearing words and phrases such as "fired" and "letter of reprimand" had created a moment of hesitation. Then Ms. Pamela Chapman, an experienced and veteran teacher, took over. Ms. Chapman intently scanned the room and said, "I thank these gentlemen for telling us about all of the possible consequences of our actions. However, I stood on the line in 1990. I was there! Dave, you were there! Theresa, you were there! Marsha, you were there! Guess what? WE ARE STILL HERE! They won't touch any of us because they can't! We can take a blue-flu day, and if we do, I'll be right there with all of you, but make no mistake about it, this will take a full-blown strike. We did it 1990. We should have done it years ago. If we want anything accomplished, we will have to do it now!" The crowd boomed in agreement. Nervous but excited, a young lady beside of me said, "This is real life. We are really going to do this, aren't we?" I looked around at my Mingo County colleagues enthusiastically approving talk of a strike and replied with full confidence, "Yes, yes we are."

There was truly only one issue left in the minds of Mingo County employees: how would the Board of Education and

Central Office react? Immediately, that question was answered. A BOE member stood to make a speech, and the crowd anxiously leaned in to hear the response to such strong discussion. The board member looked through the audience and said, "I have already made it clear that I support you and I stand with you. After listening to several speeches tonight I think I need to make something else clear. In order for anyone in this room to be fired or to receive a letter of reprimand it has to go through ME. And I would NEVER vote yes. If you are brave enough to stand, I'll be brave enough to support you!" The crowd immediately leapt to their feet as we responded with a powerful, long, and thunderous ovation. The BOE member had more to say, but the crowd didn't need to hear anything more. It was decided. We had the support of our administrators, our fellow colleagues, and now our Board of Education. We were going to create a one-day work stoppage, and we were going to be untouchable while we did it.

After listening to ten more speeches from teachers imploring the audience to stand in unity and strength, I cleared my throat and asked to speak next. "I believe it is clear that we have decided to quit talking and finally take action," I said. "However, this alone is not enough. We cannot leave this room until we decide on a date. Whether we realize it or not, the eyes of the state are on Mingo County. Right now teachers in the other fifty-four counties know that we have called this meeting. They have scheduled their own meetings later in this week, and they will chart their path based on what we choose to do here this evening. It's not enough to tell them we are going to have a one-day blue flu. We must tell them when. Will all fifty-four follow us? No. However, we don't need fifty-four. We just need a spark. If we can do this, if we can stand, then we know that our brothers and sisters in Wyoming are not going to let us stand alone. We know that our brothers and sisters in Logan County will not let us stand alone. The south WILL stand. And if the south stands, the rest of the state will follow our lead. It may take a week, two weeks, or three weeks, but they will follow Mingo County."

It was decided. Within seventy-two hours, educators all across Mingo and Wyoming counties were voting by secret ballot on a one-day work stoppage on February 2, 2018. Wyoming County titled the day "Fed Up Friday." The votes were counted, but the result was a foregone conclusion. Teachers were placing orders for red shirts that said "I Stand With Public Employees" and "RespectED." As a building-level representative, I was responsible for counting the votes for my school. There was only one surprise: four people had chosen not to mark yes or no. "Would you be willing to participate in Fed Up Friday, February 2nd, 2018?" the ballot asked. Their response? "HELL YES."

Throughout southern West Virginia, counties started holding emergency meetings and voting on "Fed Up Friday" participation. Members of the Mingo County Education Association traveled to meetings in other counties to speak on our decision and help provide courage to those who might have been afraid of joining the movement. This strategy proved effective, and many people said that if it wouldn't have been for the voice of those from Mingo and Wyoming, other counties wouldn't have considered joining. In the end, four counties voted to walk: Mingo, Wyoming, McDowell, and Logan. Initially, pushback was severe across the mountain state. Many educators said we were "hotheads," "divisive," "jumping the gun," and "impulsive." In spite of such criticism, there was never a moment of doubt or reconsideration. We knew in the south that we were not creating division; we were creating a movement. We were not under any false illusions. We didn't expect all fifty-five counties to walk out on February 2. We knew we had to provide our colleagues around the state with a spark of courage. Our blue-flu day was never intended to be the only action. It was meant to start the action.

As February 2 approached, Mingo teachers' pride and enthusiasm grew. Educators would rush into the teacher lounge and announce, "McDowell just confirmed! They are walking with us!" and everyone would start fist bumping and shouting in celebration.

We had everything we needed: red t-shirts, professionally printed signs, and the unity of four counties. There was only one problem: snow was in the forecast.

The night of February 1, we had a conference call with union leaders across the county. We went over our plan. We would wake up at 5:00 a.m. in preparation for the two-hour trek to Charleston, the state capital. With snow a possibility, we needed to prepare for a three-hour drive. We would meet at Laidley Field and march over to the capitol with colleagues from our respective schools.

At 5:00 a.m. my alarm blared, and I sleepily looked through my blinds. Three inches of snow already covered the ground, and more was on the way. Dejected, I asked my husband how many people he thought would be there. He replied, "I don't really know, but I'm terrified this will hurt our numbers. No matter what though, we will be there." Throughout the three-hour drive people from all over the southern part of the state were calling us. Based on the people we knew, the snow wasn't going to hurt our numbers. In fact, it was actually going to help. Nearby counties including Boone and Raleigh were closed due to weather, and educators from those counties were posting on social media that they were on their way to the capital. As we turned the corner and saw the parking lot for Laidley Field, we nearly lost our breath. It was absolutely packed. We couldn't see the actual crowd just yet, but it was clear that there was a massive turnout.

As we started our walk to the capitol, the support we felt was overwhelming. Everyone was honking their horn at us as a sign of support. People were stopping in the middle of the street, rolling their windows down, and telling us to "Give 'em hell." It was nineteen degrees outside, the snow still falling steadily, but we were so fired up, the cold didn't touch us.

I stood in line with teachers from my school, Mingo Central Comprehensive High School, for two and a half hours before we were permitted inside the building. We filled the time with "Fed Up, Fired Up" chants and county roll calls where someone would scream "MINGO" and everyone from Mingo would cheer. Then the chant leader would continue calling out the names of the other counties present. Despite our energy and excitement, by the time we were admitted my feet were so cold I couldn't even feel my toes. Once we cleared security I turned around and asked one of my coworkers a critical question: where were we going? The last time I was in the capitol was when I was a sophomore in high school. I didn't know where to go, and to my surprise, neither did she. In a group of over twenty educators, no one knew where to go. Finally one woman said, "Listen. Do you hear that? It sounds like chanting. Let's follow the noise."

We passed through several corridors until finally we ended up in the rotunda. The sound was deafening. There were thousands of educators at the doors of both the House and Senate chambers, standing together and chanting in unison. The sight of that sea of red brought tears to my eyes. For at least two minutes our small group of teachers just stood and soaked in the atmosphere. When we finally moved, we decided to go to the Senate chambers. At first we started chanting "We want Justice!" and "Vote them out!" Then, someone near the front started chanting "We will strike! We will strike!" and immediately the sea of red took up the rallying call and ultimatum. I looked at my closest friends, and we all looked stunned. Were we really going to declare this and draw a line in the sand? Absolutely. With more fervor and intensity than I had used in any of the previous chants, I screamed with the crowd, "We will strike!" Every time I said it, I became more convinced that this was the path we would be forced to take.

As the Senate session drew to a close and the crowd started to dissipate, my husband stood at the door of the Senate chamber, a man on a mission. I asked if he was ready to leave, and he said, "No, I'm not leaving until they HEAR me." It was clear that most senators had left through a private entrance and were not going to face the crowd. Eventually, one senator walked through the door, and my husband immediately went to him to ask questions. This

> It is our hope that the fire neither dims nor burns out but instead burns bright in educators across the United States as we stand with pride and declare,
>
> ## "We are worthy!"

senator looked at my husband and said, "Listen, if you don't like what's going on in Charleston why don't you put your ass on a damn ballot." Before my husband could even respond, his colleague fired off, "If you want to vote on education issues, why don't you get your ass in my damn classroom?" He simply walked off, and we were left with no other option but to leave the capitol. "Fed Up Friday" was over, and we were more fed up and fired up than ever before.

On the half-mile walk back to our cars, one teacher said, "We really are going to have to strike." Our silence was affirmation. We knew this day would either be a wake-up call for legislators or educators. It was clear that it had sounded the alarm across the state, and it was the educators who had chosen to respond.

The news media has reported extensively about the people and the events of 55 Strong. But before we were 55 Strong, we were Mingo County Strong. We were Southern WV Strong. The truth is, every fire starts with a spark. On January 23, in the deep dark hills of southern West Virginia, the spark was ignited. Through the tireless efforts of thousands of individuals that spark was then fanned into a flame. This flame has not only covered all of West Virginia but has spread throughout the country as educators in Kentucky, Arizona, and Oklahoma have been inspired to stand in strength and unity. It is our hope that the fire neither dims nor burns out but instead burns bright in educators across the United States as we stand with pride and declare, "We are worthy!" ✖

I live in Davis, a very small and very rural town in Tucker County. I call it the Promised Land. I gave up teaching in Maryland, **willingly took** a huge pay **cut** to move here, and I never looked back.

—Erin Marks

Erin Marks
Tucker County High School, Tucker County

**W**ait… what are they making us do now for PEIA?" I asked my secretary at work sometime back in January. Little did any of us know that conversations like this were happening all across the state as PEIA began to inform us that soon we would be required to accrue points on the Go365 platform. Soon after that conversations about the increase in monthly premiums dominated the hallways and offices. These changes would not affect me as a single and childless employee, but I knew it was about to rock the financial worlds of most of my coworkers.

I live in Davis, a very small and very rural town in Tucker County. I call it the Promised Land. I gave up teaching in Maryland, willingly took a huge pay cut to move here, and I never looked back. Not even for those nine days. These mountains have become my home and I cherish this community like none other. I would go to the ends of the earth for anyone in it, and I know that any of them would do the same for me. However, when the questions of a possible strike arose, I was scared.

I attended a meeting that was held off school grounds and after school hours to discuss what we should do. There was talk about a protest on Saturday in Charleston and a couple more in our county that week. There was even more talk about the strike back in the 90s. Tucker was one of the very first counties to go on strike, and people still remembered who continued to report to work and crossed the picket lines. By the end of the meeting I was even more scared at the idea of my close-knit staff being divided. I was petrified by the fact that I somehow was nominated to be the one to collect the vote from our staff as to who would be willing to strike or not.

That same day I collected the vote, we found out that our superintendents would support us. We would not miss a paycheck. School would just be cancelled. No one would have to cross a picket line. We would stay unified. I was elated. And with that it was decided: Tucker would not report to work on February 22 or 23. That next day I collected money from all the staff for the local food banks, because again, that is how this community rolls.

I went home and made a poster. It needed to be simple, easily read, and direct. It was a hot pink sign with black letters which read "Health not Wealth." I still remember the strange feelings I had looking at that piece of poster board. This piece of wood pulp and glue would be with me sharing my message to my community and to the state. I had never felt so proud and scared. Honestly, I cried that night. What if we didn't win? What if I let my coworkers and all the other state employees down? What if we lost the support of our board and our superintendent? What if this "got real" and we didn't get paid? What if we were divided? I didn't sleep much that night as I anticipated what to expect when I would arrive in Charleston the next day.

To explain what I saw the next day takes a small backstory. Two years ago, one of my good friends and coworkers lost her battle to cancer. She had fought for many years as it first started attacking her breasts, then her lungs, and then finally her brain. Lisa was a powerful force. She put her full heart and soul into everything for her students and staff. Many of us had made comments over those days of how much she would have loved to be a part of all this. Her energy was infectious and her drive was fierce. She died a young and painful death, and it was not fair. That first morning of the strike, February 22, I got into my car and headed to Charleston with another coworker and friend. As we stopped in Thomas for gas, a full and complete double rainbow greeted us. It was strong and it was bold. It was hard to not imagine that Lisa had something to do with it. It was hard to not have faith that we would win this fight.

Those next several days had some powerful and scary moments. I screamed at big wooden doors in those marbled hallways. I cried (I'm a crier… what can I say?) to my family and friends. I stood on the side of the road hoping that every car would honk as I continued to wave my simple hot pink sign. I bonded with my coworkers like never before so that now when I see those bus drivers cross my path in our morning drives, we share a knowing smile because we will always remember those nine days when we were all #55STRONG. ✖

Parry Casto
Explorer Academy, Cabell County

I'm a fifth-grade teacher at the Explorer Academy in Huntington, West Virginia. But you might better recognize me as the person dressed up as Uncle Sam. During the work stoppage, I helped organize and lead the chants every day at the capitol.

As the wave of dissent began accumulating and the reality of a work stoppage became imminent, it became apparent that my role as AFT building rep for Explorer Academy had to become more tangible, organized, and focused. After the authorization vote had passed county wide, Cabell, Wayne, and Mason counties agreed to a one-day work stoppage on Friday, February 16, one day ahead of the Working Families Rally at the capitol on Saturday, February 17. This day would prove to be a template as to what I would do for the next nine days at the capitol.

On February 16 and the first two days of the actual statewide stoppage, I was not dressed as Uncle Sam. Instead, I wore an all-red suit complemented by my red Chuck Taylors. On that first day, I rode to the capitol with my teacher friends from Explorer Academy. Upon entry, we quickly made our way up to the rotunda and ultimately picked the House side of the capitol to begin our protests.

You see, there really isn't a playbook by which to encourage people to participate in public dissent. You could feel an air of internal rage churning, but I felt it was lacking the power that the situation needed so I started shuffling closer toward the front of the crowd and began chanting loudly. It didn't take long for people to notice me and engage in the chants. By the end of the day, I was front and center at the steps of the House chamber entrance leading many of the chants. At that moment, I knew that for our cause to be successful, there needed to be one or multiple "cheerleaders" or "chant leaders" to help sustain a high and consistent level of outrage we all possessed. I knew my efforts would be best served by being that "rabble rouser" daily at the capitol for however long it required.

So, on the first day of the actual work stoppage, I already understood what my responsibilities would entail. Still dressed in the all-red suit, I rode up with my friends from Huntington High, where I used to work, and continued leading the chants. In addition, I knew that the power of social media could help expose our cause to a greater number of people online. Front and center on the House chamber's steps, I recorded many of the House delegates' motivational speeches that day on Facebook Live. By the end of the first day, thousands of people had viewed the Facebook Live videos and I had a multitude of shares and comments on my posts.

I clearly remember the thoughts I had leading up to me donning the Uncle Sam costume on Monday, February 22 and wearing it every day until the end of the stoppage except on Wednesday, February 24; I wore all-black that day. In the back of my brain I had always considered wearing the suit, but I was also apprehensive. I worried that if I wore the costume, it could be construed by some as a mockery of our efforts. My sole intention was that by wearing the Uncle Sam costume, I could help unite our efforts by being a symbol of justice and solidarity.

It proved to be one of the best decisions I had ever made in my life.

From the moment I wore the Uncle Sam costume at the capitol, my life changed. The thousands of people that came up to have their picture taken with me is forever imprinted upon my soul. Every time, I enthusiastically obliged and asked them what county they were from. Smiles always beamed from their faces. I believe that I met people from all of the "#55STRONG" West Virginia counties. It was such a blessing to be that positive image, voice, and inspiration to that many people in such a short period of time. It became clear by the end of the work stoppage that what I was representing was far larger than any one person or group of people could possibly comprehend. Although I became the "face" of a movement in West Virginia, it took an entire village to pull off this incredible feat. I was just one of the many cogs in place that were moving together in perfect unison.

But I cannot lie. Each day was more difficult than the previous one. A day of teaching paled in comparison to the amount of energy and effort I expended as an activist on the front line at the capitol. The daily rigors were beginning to take their toll on my body by the first full week's end. I barely had a voice left. I looked and felt haggard. I had lost almost ten pounds from the constant exercising and lack of caloric intake.

But I knew that for all my and other individuals' suffering, if we stayed consistently fervent and "#55united," we would wear down the opposing legislators in the end. If successful, this wouldn't just have a lasting effect on teachers and state employees within our own state but could be the springboard to leading a national teacher and labor movement. When the announcement finally came on Tuesday, March 6 that the Senate had agreed to sign the bill that would authorize a 5 percent pay raise for all state employees and PEIA Task Force expectations, it was probably the most satisfying emotional release of anything I've ever experienced except for the birth of my daughter. A moment of pure joy and celebration that I'll never forget. ✖

THIS WORK STOPPAGE WAS ABOUT STANDING UP AS A STATE AND TELLING OUR LEADERSHIP WHAT WE VALUE. WE VALUE OURSELVES. WE VALUE THE BLUE COLLAR, GRITTY WEST VIRGINIA WORKER. WE VALUE THE COAL MINER, THE TRUCK DRIVER, THE TEACHER.

—Mark Salfia

Mark Salfia
Shepherdstown Middle School, Jefferson County

My experience during the work stoppage was unique. On January 3 I had just started a new job as assistant principal at Shepherdstown Middle School, making me probably the least experienced administrator in West Virginia. I had just left my job as a classroom teacher where for fifteen years I had taught U.S. history and civics, coached baseball, and for the last four had served as the social studies department chair at Spring Mills High School, where I had built relationships with the faculty and staff. The folks at Spring Mills knew me. They knew my wife and kids, my likes and dislikes, my strengths and weaknesses. But most importantly they knew they could trust me. At Shepherdstown I was the outsider.

As a brand new administrator, I suddenly found myself on both sides of the issue. I very strongly believed in the fight and I knew the only way we would win is if we stuck together and were willing to stay out as long as necessary. But my problem now was, my role was different. I would be required to go to work regardless of how long the strike lasted. I would have to be there to open up the building in case students had nowhere else to go, and the part I worried about most, to allow the teachers who decided to cross picket lines an opportunity to work. I had spoken to my wife about donating my salary to charity or to the school's faculty senate fund if it got to that point, as a show of unity with my colleagues, but I still couldn't help but wonder if the people I was standing alongside would view me as a hypocrite.

To show solidarity, the first thing I did every morning during the work stoppage was send an email to the faculty telling them I was proud to work with them. I spent as much time out on the picket lines as I could, which went a long way toward building trust. Those were long, stressful, nervous days, but I was energized by the passion and resolve that I saw from teachers all across the state. A lot of my current and former colleagues were asking me for advice on what to do next, or what I thought would happen. And I knew we were doing the right thing and I was proud to be a part of it. It was easy for me to encourage them to keep fighting, but I couldn't help but think: Why do we have to? Why in 2018 do workers in West Virginia still not have the respect they deserve?

For me the work stoppage was a fight over what we value. West Virginia labor has a long and proud history of fighting for what is right. This was never more evident than back in the early 1900s, when coal was king and the coal bosses controlled the state. This spilled over dramatically in the Battle of Blair Mountain, where the miners of Mingo County fought bravely and proudly against the bosses and their hired guns. History remembers the miners as heroes who fought for what they knew was right, but the truth is they lost and the money won. The coal bosses, many of them from out of state, continued to be some of the richest men in the country while the miners, and, really the entire state, remained dependent on a product that was dangerous to get to, hazardous to breathe, and destructive to our land and water. Surrounding states found new and more creative ways to make money and employ their residents, while West Virginia remained stuck in the same cycle it had been in for decades.

Fast forward to the present day, and it's all happening again. We have been told West Virginia is "the Saudi Arabia of natural gas." Out-of-state companies are coming in, destroying our land, taking our gas, and making millions of dollars. It's created a handful of jobs for West Virginians, but for the most part all the real money is going out of state. The leadership of our state, scared to spook away any business at all in a fragile economy, has chosen to value the quick economic boost from these out-of-state companies, knowing full well they'll leave when the well dries up, leaving behind another generation of poverty. They are taxed next to nothing, costing us valuable dollars that could be used to invest in the future of West Virginia. This work stoppage was about standing up as a state and telling our leadership what we value. We value ourselves. We value the blue collar, gritty West Virginia worker. We value the coal miner, the truck driver, the teacher. This started out as a teacher and service personnel walk out, but make no mistake it turned into a labor movement. The 5 percent pay raise was an arbitrary number, and all of us know we are worth way more than that anyway. This movement was about being valued. The working class across our state, and really across the whole country, took notice.

Going back in to Shepherdstown Middle School the day after the strike ended was one of the best days I've had in fifteen years of education. We played music and lined up at the front door to greet every kid who walked in. They high-fived us and hugged us. I get chills just thinking about it. I think all of us, not only at Shepherdstown but around the state, have a newfound respect for one another. We stood united fighting for the future of West Virginia just as our ancestors had done at Blair Mountain. I am proud to have been a part of it. ✖

Brandon Wolford
Lenore K-8, Mingo County

Growing up in the coalfields of Kentucky and West Virginia, I was well acquainted at an early age with the impact labor movements had on the working class. I vividly recall sitting in front of the television for hours watching low-quality VHS tapes of the coal miners' strike that had occurred in Appalachia over a period of four years during the mid-1980s. Although the strike had occurred before my time, my father had participated in the movement, and my mother had kept detailed footage of the events as they unfolded. Knowing the role my father and both grandfathers had played in these events sparked a special interest. I wanted to be involved in a movement like that one day. "It would be so much fun," I remember thinking. It would be several years later that I found out my original thoughts were far from the truth. It is also fair to say that I soon learned the true meaning behind the labor movements in Appalachia—it is not strictly about the contracts, wages, or benefits; it is something much deeper. Those people had fought for the dignity they so rightfully deserved, and together they stood in unity as brothers and sisters.

When I became a teenager, I realized just how deeply the union roots ran in our family. My great-grandfather, K.B. Dixon, an orphan from Statesville, North Carolina, is a prime example. There was a time in the 1920s, while down on his luck, that K. B. decided to board a train without purchasing a ticket. In doing so, my great-grandfather became one of the many hobos of that era. At the time he had no real destination in mind. He simply wanted a new start in life. Unbeknownst to K. B., the train's destination was a small mining community in Mingo County, West Virginia, called Chattaroy.

Desperate for work, K. B. eagerly accepted the first offer of employment he received, which turned out to be a job in the coal mines. Oddly enough, and much to his surprise, once he reported for duty he was unable to communicate successfully with the other miners. Most of his fellow miners were Italian immigrants who spoke little English, and sometimes none at all. Curious as to why there were no other English-speaking employees, great-grandpa made some inquiries and discovered that he had unknowingly crossed a picket line, making him a "scab." He immediately walked off the job and joined the UMWA in their efforts for better wages and living conditions. Great-grandpa would go on to become part of the first major union organization in United States history, participating in the mine wars in and around the town of Matewan, West Virginia. He remained a miner in the Appalachian Mountains, and eventually became president of local UMWA 1440. During this time he met and worked with John L. Lewis, one of the first, and, in the opinion of many, the most effective leader of organized labor in American history. Lewis helped pave the way for many of the unions that exist today across our nation.

Unfortunately, my great-grandfather, K.B. Dixon, did not live to see the results of his efforts on future generations. He was killed in a slate fall inside the mines at the age of forty-six.

I learned of the existence of teacher unions in West Virginia only after I myself became a teacher. Shortly after I started my first job, a lady approached me with a membership form and calendar. "Would you like to join our teachers' union, the WVEA?" she asked. Fully aware of my heritage, I quickly responded, "Yes."

The union was invaluable to me in my early years as a teacher. Back then, I still struggled to become a better educator, and was eager for mentorship and guidance, but it was hard to find. When I was forced to file a grievance against an administrator who had denied me a job, the union had my back—and this experience, which was ultimately resolved, led to me getting involved in the Mingo County Education Association. Shortly after I started attending meetings I was voted in as president of that association, and I made a vow to serve the teachers in Mingo County to the very best of my ability, even those not in the union.

My life as a teacher went fairly smoothly for the next few years. Everyone around our county seemed satisfied with the wages they were receiving. Across the border in Kentucky teachers were making five to seven thousand dollars more than in West Virginia, but the major perk of teaching in West Virginia at that time was the healthcare benefits. West Virginia had one of the best systems, in my opinion. Kentucky and some other states had higher premiums and less coverage. Therefore, it was my understanding that lower wages were not an issue so long as the PEIA insurance compensated the difference.

Although I tried to maintain an active WVEA local union, it was dormant for the most part. We were lucky if we had ten to fifteen members in attendance at a meeting, and even then it was only if they were experiencing a problem. Then, in 2012, our state legislature began discussing teachers' pay and comparing it to other states. Realizing that West Virginia was one of the lowest on the pay scale, they made a vow to make our wages more competitive. The promise was to have the starting salary for a first year teacher increased from the state minimum of approximately $30,000 to $43,000 by the year 2019, with a $1,000.00 raise the first year. This would be followed by $2,000 increments added every year thereafter until 2019. Needless to say, we received the one-time raise of $1,000 the very first year and not an additional penny over the next seven years.

Sometime around 2015 the frustrations in the school system started to build in our county, as well as in the state. It became apparent that the days of quality insurance would soon come to an end. Premiums slowly began to rise, while the PEIA introduced a new program called "Healthy Tomorrows." This included a form which required every employee to visit a physician for a check-up. If one's waist size, blood pressure, height, weight, cholesterol, or any other factor determined by the insurance company to be relevant did not match the numbers they felt were acceptable, a $500 penalty was placed on out-of-pocket deductible for those who did not meet the set criteria. The "Healthy Tomorrows" program continued each year as premiums continued to rise and the quality of coverage drastically decreased. It soon became clear that the state was monopolizing the insurance and attempting to force everyone to use hospitals within the borders of West Virginia. Living on the border, it was a shorter drive for me to go to a Kentucky hospital twenty miles away when I suspected that I had a kidney stone. A simple scan confirmed several small kidney stones and a prescription was issued. I was released after a few hours in the emergency room. No surgery was required and there were no complications. Nonetheless, PEIA claimed the hospital I used was out of network. They paid very little, and I was left with a bill of $1,800 for a simple emergency room visit. God forbid it had turned out to be something serious.

As a teacher and union leader, I heard increasing complaints concerning PEIA coverage and premiums each year whenever staff members and their families needed medical attention. I felt as if it was going to eventually come to a point that PEIA went bankrupt, or we would have to drop the insurance altogether due to poor coverage. Then came the meetings of the PEIA board in late 2017, which would eventually awaken the sleeping giant that had remained silent in our state for nearly eighty years.

Unbeknownst to most educators and public employees until this time, the legislature itself did not make specific decisions concerning PEIA. The detailed requirements and premiums, in addition to programs such as "Healthy Tomorrows," were made at the discretion of nine PEIA board members, each of whom serve four-year terms and are appointed by the governor. On December 7, 2017, the board announced that, beginning July 1, 2018, all employees would be required to enroll in a Humana program known as "Go365." Under this program, all public employees who carried PEIA would have to wear a device like a Fitbit, which would log one's daily steps. The program would require each policyholder to meet a certain number of steps per day and month.

They would then be able to earn points based on meeting a specific goal determined by the PEIA board. If those goals were met, he or she would receive rewards such as a gift card to a retail store or an online service. However, those who failed to meet the criteria, or refused to participate in the program, would be penalized $25 per month in addition to the set premiums, which were also scheduled to rise, yet again, beginning the next fiscal year.

Along with Go365, the board also approved to change the number of tiers which would determine employee premiums, reducing the number of tiers from ten down to five, resulting in a major increase across the board for all employees. However, although teachers were outraged by the first two changes, it seemed that the third change approved was the one that had everyone the most upset. While in the past, public employees' insurance premiums had always been based on the individual policyholder's salary, the board voted to require all those covered under each policy to report his or her wages to the board, including a spouse and children. For instance, if a female teacher had her husband covered on her insurance plan, along with two teenage children with part-time jobs, all four individuals would be required to report their earnings, and the premium would be determined based on total household income. For most families, this change alone would have made insurance premiums skyrocket to the point where most would not benefit financially to work at all.

While the PEIA board approved all the amendments, they were not immediately publicized around the state. Our union leaders attempted to bring those changes to our attention, but not everyone took the time to educate themselves on what was really happening. It even took me a while to develop a full understanding of what was happening. We had remained silent for so long and had accepted whatever the state had thrown our way that I think everyone felt hopeless. We were the forgotten employees, our voices would never be heard, and we could never generate enough momentum to make a difference, even if we tried.

I, too, shared this belief. While always willing to stand, I had noticed a common sense of fear among coworkers at the building and county level over my years in Mingo County Schools. Most were afraid to speak up. They feared retaliation if they made waves. Some teachers were to the point of never speaking up for themselves because they feared the possibility of termination. When given the opportunity, and because I was known as one of the most outspoken employees in the county, I would reply to these individuals who were afraid to take a stand by saying, "They haven't fired me yet, so you shouldn't have anything to worry about."

Less than one month after the PEIA decision was made, the West Virginia Education Association called for all members to rally at the capitol in opposition to the PEIA changes. Once again, most of us did not fully understand the severity of what was happening, so only a handful attended the rally. I did not attend. "No one will stand with us. People are job-scared, so I'm wasting my day by going," I recall thinking, and I am sure that is the attitude most employees across the state had at that time.

Luckily, a small group of teachers from the Gilbert area in our county did attend the meeting, including Justin Endicott, Stephanie Endicott, Kathy Woodruff, Naomi Cline, and Becky Endicott. Upon their return from the capitol, they informed me of the severity of the events unfolding in Charleston. Not only were legislators attacking our insurance, but several other legislative bills had been proposed that would negatively affect the teaching profession if approved.

Legislation was being introduced by the Republican Party, for example, that would eliminate seniority in the reduction and transfer process altogether. That law, if passed, would have allowed principals and superintendents to choose who they wanted to remain in the schools from year to year. If the county was paying a large salary to a thirty-year educator, that bill would have allowed that educator to be laid off, while retaining a position for a first-year teacher earning significantly less. I was also informed of a bill under consideration that would add to our already-skyrocketing insurance premiums. Thirdly, a bill was proposed that would defund public education by allocating the resources from the already bare-bones budget over into charter schools. Not only would such an act cause more educators to leave West Virginia, but it would also make it impossible to pay teachers, provide resources for our students in the public sector, and thus, create an even more negative learning environment across the state than we already had. In an attempt to somewhat camouflage the insurance issue, legislators were pushing a bill that would promise teachers a 1 percent raise each year over the next five years; which would equal about $404, per year. When I heard about these proposals, I exclaimed, "What's going on here? This is much bigger than I initially anticipated."

On January 17, 2018, Senator Richard Ojeda stood on the floor in open session and proclaimed, "Instead of 1 percent or 2 percent raise, how about a $2,000 raise this year, and next year, and the next year? " words to that effect. The senator went on to say, "But I'm telling you right now, this 1 percent and 2 percent is a slap in their face, and I'm telling you, we're sitting on a powder keg. If you do not think that the teachers across our state right now are saying the 's' word, you're wrong!" Senator Ojeda's remarks renewed a sense of hope in employees across the state who had felt forgotten for a number of years.

Within a day or two, I was contacted by our local WVEA representative, Mr. Allen Stump. He informed me that our neighboring local in Wyoming County was going to meet within the next few days in an attempt to organize an event they had deemed "Fed Up Friday." This was to be held on February 2, 2018, and all members were going to march on the capitol in Charleston, if approved by a majority vote. "OK," I thought, "We need to do something like this in Mingo as well." I immediately scheduled an emergency meeting on January 23, 2018, at the Carewood Facility in Delbarton. To my surprise, Senator Ojeda was one of the first politicians to say, "I'll be there."

At the same time, for the first time in state history, the two largest unions in our state, WVEA and AFT, decided to lock arms and stand together as one in the fight. We had approximately 200 employees at that meeting. There were several guest speakers in addition to Senator Ojeda, including two board members. A sense of shock filled the room as each individual attack on education was addressed. Our local union representatives from both organizations were in attendance. It soon became apparent that our state leaders were discouraging the union reps from supporting a walkout. My people were furious. Finally, I stood up and said, "I was elected by you, these gentlemen standing up here are paid by you, and whatever the majority wants to do, we will do!" At that point several members from the audience spoke, and the overwhelming majority approved a motion to participate in "Fed Up Friday." Although the idea was conceived in Wyoming County, we beat them to the vote by one day, making Mingo County the first to initially declare a Strike Day in the state.

The next day, the superintendent informed our organization that an official vote would need to be taken to determine if enough employees were planning to participate in the event before he would cancel school. Building representatives were appointed at each worksite, and Mingo County had an overwhelming 87.5 percent of its professional employees on board. School was cancelled on February 2, 2018.

Wyoming County followed the same procedure as "Fed Up Friday," which had initially been their idea. Then, it was time to encourage others to get on board. Our neighboring county of Logan held a similar meeting on January 31, 2018. I, along with the four of the Gilbert teachers, attended the meeting. We experienced the same reaction from our state representatives there, too. There was not much encouragement to strike, but the difference, in my opinion, between the Logan County meeting and our meeting was the fact that the president of their local did not seem to want to listen to his people.

The building was packed, even more so than the Mingo County meeting. People were angry. They wanted to take action. Yet, the leadership was telling them, "We will only make the third county to go out. We need to wait. Three counties in a state of fifty-five will not amount to anything." Observing the members' dismay, I stood a few times and spoke to the membership as a whole. I reminded them that the leaders as well as the officers had to go with the majority vote, so all they needed to do was to make a motion to participate in "Fed Up Friday."

Later, I reminded the members of a situation that had been brought to my attention recently that had occurred in the early 2000s in Monongalia County, where teachers did a one-day "walk-out" and it resulted in a $2,000 raise for everyone. I said to them, "If they can get $2,000 by striking for one day, with only one county in the state participating, imagine what we can do with three counties!" It was at this point that the membership seemed to take control of the meeting, and Logan County soon voted. They were on board for "Fed Up Friday" as well. Not long after, I was given a directive to stay in my own local, and not attend meetings in any other county. Apparently, a few individuals did not like what I said, but I disagreed. I am for the people, especially the teachers with whom I work, and who I represent. I believe it is the responsibility of any officer to stand with the majority, regardless of personal opinion. By the time "Fed Up Friday" rolled around, we had six or seven counties willing to participate.

The teachers in Mingo County returned to school the following Monday, and, by the next day, word had spread that several other counties were closing for the day to conduct another rally at the capitol. Late in the evening of February 5, 2018, I received a message that Governor Justice was planning to secretly visit our neighboring county of Logan the following morning. This meeting had not been publicized whatsoever. Principals were told to send their faculty senate president, along with one "level-headed" teacher and one "level-headed" service employee from each school to the city of Logan the following day. These "level-headed" individuals were not aware of where they were going. Being the transparent "troublemaker" that I am, I made some calls around the state, and I soon learned that the governor was indeed scheduled to go to Logan the following morning at 11:30 a.m. Coincidentally, the president of the Logan County Board of Education, Mr. Paul Hardesty, was a lobbyist for Governor Justice in Charleston, and was on his payroll earning somewhere between $500,000 to $1,000,000 per year. Mr. Hardesty had set this meeting up, in my opinion, to intimidate the teachers in Logan County, and, perhaps, to use his position to convince them to back away from the strike.

After I received confirmation of the meeting from three credible sources, I posted on three separate Facebook groups that I had learned of a secret meeting scheduled the following morning in Logan County and that Governor Justice would be speaking there. Immediately, in one group, the post was deleted because I was accused of "endangering" the governor's life. In another group, controlled by the Logan County Education Association, the post was removed as well. I received a message from one of the officers telling me that I should not post rumors, and that if it was true, I needed to allow Governor Justice to speak to the people and, hopefully, reach a resolution. In the meantime, I received calls that Mr. Hardesty had gotten wind of my post and was not happy with it.

The governor's office was going crazy in Charleston trying to get out a last-minute press release announcing the meeting for the following morning. Just as I had posted, Governor Justice was there the next morning, along with his faithful sidekick, Paul Hardesty, who stood up in an open televised meeting and attempted to clear his name. Mr. Hardesty stated, "Someone last night from Mingo County, Mr. Wolford, said we tried to have a secret meeting here in Logan today. Ladies and gentlemen, there's nothing about me that's secret. I'm six foot eight and I weigh three hundred pounds." Of course, there was no response; this was their board president. Employees were afraid to speak up in fear of retaliation. The people knew I had been honest in my post. I had no reason to lie. As for their intent in keeping the meeting a secret, it just goes to show one how politicians work. The majority are only going to look after their own interests, and, in the case of Mr. Hardesty, he was looking out for the best interest of his buddy, Governor Justice, who had lined his pockets for years. It was also at this meeting that Governor Justice made one of the most critical remarks of his career. Remember how Senator Ojeda stood with the teachers from day one by making his comments on the senate floor? Well, Governor Justice had some choice words for him as well, addressing the teachers by saying, "If you choose to respond to somebody that's a politician, that's running around through the streets and didn't stand with you anymore than I could fly through the sky— then you're being 'dumb bunnies.' "

WVEA leadership informed the local presidents, via a conference call, that they, along with AFT leadership, had decided to take a strike authorization vote across the state in which every employee, union and non-union, were to be polled. The vote was held across the state during the week of February 6, 2018. We were given instructions to report to a statewide meeting in Flatwoods, WV on February 11, 2018, to present the results.

It was at this time that I created a local Facebook Messenger group with one or two building representatives from all schools in Mingo County. Rather than posting potentially damaging messages via Facebook, I began hosting calls almost nightly. We set up the method in which the strike authorization votes would be collected. To ensure that our numbers were not skewed, each building representative was issued a list of all employees within his or her building, along with color coded ballots, with each school being issued a different color. A sealed box was assigned to each building and the ballots were submitted in a manner in which they could not be removed. One by one, each school returned their ballots and a few members from different locations were assigned to tally the votes. One individual was not solely authorized to count all the school votes, in order to prevent an estimate from being calculated. Once this information was reported to the organization, I tallied the votes and did not release the overall results until the meeting in Flatwoods. Out of 511 Mingo County employees participating in the vote, 433, a startling 85 percent, voted in favor of authorizing a strike. It became apparent that all the other counties, for the most part, were in agreement and shared the same feelings as Mingo County. We were definitely 55 Strong!

On February 13, 2018, more walkouts continued across the state, this time with Cabell, Lincoln, and Wayne counties joining with the others. Then, at a Saturday rally on the capitol steps on February 17, 2018, our state leaders, Dale Lee and Christine Campbell, announced for a statewide work stoppage to be effective the following Thursday and Friday—February 22 and 23, 2018. While many of us were excited to hear this announcement, a large percentage was afraid of losing the only source of income they had. Some households, including mine, were held together strictly based on teachers' salaries. In an attempt to ease the anxiety, I spoke with my longtime friend and coworker, Debbie Sheppard, who works in the Mingo County Federal Credit Union. Sheppard assured me that, in the event that school was not cancelled, she would work overtime to help all eligible employees obtain small loans. Employees could pay these loans back once the strike was over. This helped our members to feel more secure about their finances in the event that it came down to an all-out strike.

February 22, 2018, marked the beginning of a nine-day war at the capitol, which would eventually end in victory. I continued my daily calls with WVEA state leaders, followed by local calls with building representatives. One of the key factors in union organization, I learned, was communication. Our building representatives reported to each employee at their work location, who, in turn, reported to me, and we determined a consensus at each county level before I reported to the state leaders. In order to maintain public support, and to allow everyone to take part in the fight, we scheduled various rallying points in the county, while assigning others to the capitol, and then we alternated days. To say we were not welcome at the capitol would be an understatement. Senator Mitch Carmichael continued to smirk and make crude remarks about teachers. At one point Senator Carmichael accused teachers of "Depriving students of the one hot meal they receive each day." This statement by Senator Carmichael infuriated me. Senator Carmichael is not concerned about feeding children. How many food pantries has he ever helped? What does he do to feed students through the summer? Summer break lasts much longer than the strike. Of course, this was one of many conniving tactics he and his party used in an attempt to make us appear as villains to the public.

The entire Democratic Party seemed to be standing with the teachers, while the majority of the Republicans bashed teachers and their efforts daily, telling us to "Go back to work," and, at times, laughing in our faces. But, we did not back down. One of the remarkable Republicans who stood with us and crossed party lines was Mingo County's own, Delegate Mark Dean. Justin Marcum, who represents the area where I live in Mingo County, a delegate on the Democratic ticket, stood with us as well. However, the most arrogant, shameless senator, next to Carmichael, was Wayne County's Mark Maynard, who also represents the district in Mingo County where I reside. He made several damning Facebook posts, as well as negative statements during the strike.

One evening, when I had heard enough, I responded to Maynard's post, only to have his political cronies come to his defense. Maynard immediately blocked me on social media, but I had a friend, who is also my local vice president, Wendy Barker, contact him and ask if she could meet him at the capitol the following day. I went along. Upon meeting Maynard, he wanted to shake hands and we introduced ourselves. I said "I'm Brandon Wolford, the one you blocked on Facebook last night." Stunned, he quickly responded "Well, you were a little hateful and I have a daughter on Facebook. I don't want her reading those kinds of things." I said to him, "OK, so I was blocked, yet you left the posts on there that were cursing me in your defense. Why?" Needless to say, I did not receive an answer to that question. Wendy, as well as Mingo County board member Sabrina Grace, continued to discuss the needs of the teachers. Maynard, in my opinion, was pretending to be concerned. I had heard all I cared to hear.

"Mr. Maynard," I interrupted, "Why is it that you are failing to listen to your constituents regarding the demands of the teachers?"

"Teachers only represent a small portion of those I am elected to represent," replied Maynard. "I am here to do what is right, not to get re-elected!"

"Well, it's certainly a good thing you aren't!" I responded.

Maynard turned and darted into the nearest room, saying as he went, "Thanks for your enthusiasm!"

We pressed forward several more days at the capitol with very little response. Governor Justice was still refusing to give us anything more than a 1-2 percent raise, and he was still expecting us to accept it, while the increases in PEIA would far exceed the raise he was proposing. In the meantime, those "dumb bunnies," as he had called them, began marching around the capitol in bunny costumes. We chanted, we intimidated, we smirked right back at them, but we did it in a peaceful manner, only to get home each evening and hear the majority of the Republican Party speak about the disrespect they were being shown each day at the capitol. I begged to differ. We were the ones to whom disrespect was being shown. In retaliation to our rallies at the capitol, the Republican Party drafted a bill while we were there known as "Payroll Authorization Deductions," for union members. They were proposing that, in order to remain a member of a union, all West Virginia employees would have to sign a new document each year reauthorizing unions to continue to deduct dues from their checks. This was a blatant attempt to break our unions across the state, which resulted in further outrage on behalf of the teachers.

Meanwhile, all local boards of education signed proclamations in support of the teachers. Our superintendents jumped on board as well, stating that they were going to continue to cancel school until common ground could be reached between teachers and legislatures. Our superintendent, Mr. Don Spence, was extremely supportive during the negotiations. He and I spoke daily, and he did everything in his power to ensure that every decision made at the county level was in the best interests of his teachers and students.

Finally, on March 1, 2018, Governor Justice brought forth a proposal, including a promise of freezing PEIA for seventeen months using $29 million from the rainy day fund (meaning our insurance premiums would not change), a 5 percent pay increase for all teachers (approximately $2,000 per teacher), creation of a PEIA task force that would strive to fully fund our insurance during the freeze, and removal of all bills that we considered attacks on education (seniority elimination, 60/40 out-of-pocket insurance premiums, charter schools bill, and payroll authorization). Feeling as if he had met all of our demands, Governor Justice declared March 2, 2018 a "cooling off day," for teachers, and insisted that we return to work on Monday, March 5, 2018. There was only one problem. We did not have anything in writing. Governor Justice was asking us to take his word. We had heard this before. We did not fall for it before, and we were not going to this time, either.

I called another emergency meeting in Mingo County, which was held at the Opry House in Delbarton on the same day. Our main concern was, as we had said before, no one in Mingo County trusted Governor Justice at this point. Everyone stood and voiced their concerns about reporting back to work on Monday, and only a handful of the nearly 200 in attendance agreed that we should take Governor Justice's promise seriously. So, another vote was taken., and 181 out of 190 in attendance vowed to remain on strike until the house and senate had approved Justice's promises. Meanwhile, other counties around the state were doing the same thing. I had invited Superintendent Spence to join us at the end of the meeting, where I presented him with the results of the vote. Shortly thereafter, he cancelled school. Looking back, had we not made the decision to stay out, I do not believe the promise would have been kept.

The house quickly passed all of the governor's proposals. However, Senate President Carmichael, wanting the last word, made it known that he was only going to approve a 4 percent raise. At this point it was not about the extra 1 percent, it was the principle of the matter. Governor Justice had made a promise to us, and we were going to hold him accountable. The local rallies and marches on the capitol continued for two more days the following week before the senate finally agreed to give teachers and all other state employees a 5 percent raise, along with all the other promises Governor Justice had made several days beforehand.

In conclusion, I believe all West Virginia teachers have learned a valuable lesson. It is vital that we stay informed, remain involved, and never get too comfortable with the status quo. This movement began to counteract the greed, power, and dishonesty of the Republican Party. We must remain alert, stand our ground, and never fail to rise up against those forces that seem to be hovering always near, ready to move against those who have let down their guard, who believe that it is best to let situations continue as they are, or who are too afraid of what they might lose if they speak out. We must remember who we are. We are Americans. Our constitution guarantees us certain rights, but we in the West Virginia school system know only too well how quickly those rights can be taken away. Let us remember the words of one of our founding fathers, Benjamin Franklin, who said, "We must, indeed, all hang together or, most assuredly, we shall all hang separately." ✖

"We must, indeed, all hang together or, most assuredly, we shall all hang separately."

—Benjamin Franklin

MEMBER ONE: I'm here to support the teachers and also for our PEIA-- I'm a state employee and we don't make very much, I mean if I wasn't married, I could apply and get food stamps, because of our pay.

MEMBER TWO: Did you ask her how much money she made last year? Twenty-three plus years as a full-time state employee, PLUS, she had three years temp service before she got hired on full-time-- she grossed $23,000 last year and they raised her insurance. Now that is sad. A 23 year loyal-- a twenty-three-year loyal employee. Not only that-- what they've done to the PEIA? This raise is just a slap in the face is what it is. They don't care about us. All they care about is their private personal agendas and pushing it through behind closed doors. We had Republicans that were siding with us-- they recessed, took 'em in the back room, and when they came out, they voted with their party. I mean it's sad. And what they've done with the right to work and repealing prevailing wage? I went out on a job last week, and I've been working pipeline, and they gave me a raise on the pipeline. I went out on a road job last week, and I took a dollar-fifty cut and the company didn't have to pay in my annuity, you know why? Because of no prevailing wage. And that's ridiculous! It's sad. It's sad.

65

Robin Ellis
Mingo Central Comprehensive High, Mingo County

Merriam-Webster defines the term *strike* as "a work stoppage by a body of workers to enforce compliance with demands made on an employer." Being a Mingo County native and lifelong resident, I have heard this term regarding work stoppages my whole life. After all, Mingo is the home of historic labor wars such as the Matewan Massacre, Bloody Mingo, and the Battle of Blair Mountain, to name a few. These famous—or perhaps infamous—struggles are a huge part of my Southern West Virginia heritage. The courageous spirit demonstrated by miners and their families in the face of shameless repression was and continues to be a source of inspiration to those bearing the burden of the working class. My daddy was a member of the United Mine Workers of America (UMWA) and participated in multiple strikes during my childhood. My husband, a UMWA retiree, has also participated in his fair share of intense labor conflicts. Despite such history and examples to follow, did I ever imagine that I would participate in a work stoppage? No! I did not! Did I ever anticipate that I would help lead an effort that would result in an "all in or nothing" wildcat strike? Definitely not! Am I happy that I did? You better believe it!

While the realization of an official work stoppage started to sink in on February 2 during the "Fed-Up Friday" rally, amidst chants of "WE WILL STRIKE! WE WILL STRIKE!" serious statewide voting for a work stoppage did not occur until more than a week later. By late February the idea of striking didn't bother me as much as the rumored "rolling strike" that union officials were mulling. A proposed rolling strike would have a few counties walking out each day. I didn't like the idea. What were we going to do? Only strike when it was our turn? Strike only on the days that we were given *permission* to do so? This idea seemed, well, ridiculous. I turned to my husband Donnie for his opinion, and he was quick and firm with his response: "You don't want to do that." He explained that what we were calling a "rolling strike" was what the UMWA termed a "selective strike," and in his experience selective striking was never successful. In fact, he stated that it actually weakened their efforts and that more importantly, caused serious divisions.

"It's got to be all-in or nothing," he said. Donnie understands strikes and understands what makes some successful while others fail, so I listened and shared his insight with peers and coworkers. I even emailed state and regional union representatives expressing my frustration and disappointment with the idea and my hope that they listen to the voices of their members who were clearly opposed to striking in this manner. I went on to voice my concerns that such actions would be counterproductive and detrimental to our cause. Much to my relief—and even my husband's—a rolling strike never materialized and every single school in every single county stood 55 Strong for nine days.

The first three days of the strike went by like a blur. Between local rallies and protests at the capitol I was feeling emotional and a bit overwhelmed. I didn't realize it at the time, but this entire experience was shaping up to be a textbook example of a concept which I faithfully teach my English students: Freytag's pyramid plot structure. On the afternoon of February 27—day four of the strike—I was in the thick of the rising action. Side by side with my coworkers, I was enthusiastically rallying in my hometown, stopping cars to give drivers handouts outlining our issues and offering an explanation as to why we were standing in the middle of the road holding signs rather than standing in our classrooms giving lectures. I had no idea that the climax—the emotionally intense turning point—would occur in just a few short hours.

The defining moment for me came with the announcement by Governor Jim Justice that same evening around 6:00 p.m. just before *NBC Nightly News* was scheduled to open live at the capitol in

Charleston. As I stood in my living room, eyes glued to the television, phone in hand texting my closest teacher friends, I remember thinking to myself that this couldn't be the end and that the governor, who had just the day before stated there would be consequences for our actions, would not give in so quickly, so easily. However, when he started speaking I began to think that he was doing just that! He said that teachers and education-related personnel would receive a 5 percent raise and all other state employees would receive 3 percent. In addition, a task force would be appointed to search for a long-term solution to fund our insurance program, PEIA. The following day, Wednesday, was designated as a cooling off day and we would be back in our classrooms with our students on Thursday.

We had won! Hallelujah! We had won!

Immediately, I could feel a small piece of my dignity and self-respect returning. In that moment I was overjoyed! I screamed. I yelled. I cried. I remember triumphantly text messaging my daughter and son. In that moment I felt vindicated. This feeling lasted, however, only for that moment. I soon had questions about this agreement that had been made between my union and the governor. In my ignorance and desire to feel justified I had failed to read between the lines, had failed to understand the true message, had failed to interpret the unfairness of this agreement. Once I recognized this so-called "deal" could actually harm our cause and that the promise to look into funding PEIA was just that, a promise, I started to feel angry. Angry with the governor, angry with the unions, and angry with myself. I had become complacent. For nearly twenty years I faithfully paid my union dues believing that it was the job of those whom my dues paid to look out for my best interests. A wave of disillusionment washed over me.

How could I have been so naïve? How could I have let myself be so fooled?

The adage, "Fool me once, shame on you. Fool me twice, shame on me" played in my head over and over. I was a National Board Certified teacher, for goodness sakes, and I had been duped! I was ashamed that my gullibility and ignorance of the issues had led to me to this point and was determined to now understand as much as possible as quickly as possible. I remember sitting up the entire night investigating my concerns, pondering the bold UMWA strikers who had blazed this trail for me, and praying what to do about it all. Tomorrow was a new day at the capitol and I was going to make it count.

I have often used the word epic to describe the events of day five, February 28, better known as "Cool Off Wednesday." I laugh when I think of it now because it was anything but a cooling off. In fact, this was the day I rediscovered my voice and shed the burden that complacency sometimes brings. I spoke with union officials, delegates, and the press. I asked questions. I campaigned for our cause. I stood beside my dearest friends and coworkers and chanted with a new intensity. I became an activist. This was a movement and we were a part of history.

Our scheduled return date was still slated for tomorrow, so late in the afternoon we learned that unions were asking for another vote. Many counties even voted on the steps of the capitol but before doing so, looked to Mingo County—those who had initiated the movement to begin with—to see how we would vote. More than once throughout the afternoon, representatives from other counties came to us and asked, "What's Mingo doing?" My heart filled with pride at this question: Just as Mingo had led the mine wars so many years ago, Mingo teachers were now leading what has been dubbed the "mind wars" and I couldn't be prouder.

As so many other times during this movement, things changed quickly and on March 1, day six, we were yet again faced with the responsibility of a vote to continue the strike or return to our schools. This time, unions were suggesting a return. This was a fact that concerned me as well as others. On the morning of the vote, I received multiple text messages from worried friends expressing a dread that the vote in Mingo would be to return as a gesture of good faith to the governor as well as our unions and county superintendent. My fellow Mingo Countians were in no way afraid of the next steps, but simply doing what comes naturally to us in Southern West Virginia: showing respect to those in a position of authority. I remember realizing in that moment that others had not had their "awakening" as I had. They did not truly understand, just as I had not just a few days earlier. My mind went back to the evening of my epiphany and all I could think was, *"We started this movement. We must finish it,"* while a voice deep within shouted, *"You must speak! You must make them understand the scope of this crusade! You must wake them from their complacency."* I fought this declaration, but with less than two hours before the meeting, requested and was granted time to speak.

Photo: unknown

"Will the lesson be that those in powerful positions ultimately have all the power or that the power of the people is stronger than a flawed system?"

I didn't know what I was going to say and even today describe the experience as an "out of body" one. With a passion and fervor that I had never known before, I stood before the audience of around two hundred to explain that as Mingo Countians, we had a responsibility to see the movement through to nothing short of a decided victory. I emphasized that this responsibility is not only to ourselves, but also to our county, to our state, to our nation, and most importantly, to our children. We must not falter at such a critical juncture. As I looked into the eyes of the dedicated men and women who transport, feed, educate, and nurture our young people, I became invigorated and renewed driving home the point that that this movement was historical by asking, "How do we want history to reflect *our* actions? As those who led a historic movement and *almost* won but surrendered when the challenges mounted, or as those who boldly and courageously fought the injustices of a corrupt system and never wavered to become victorious?" I challenged them to reflect on the lessons we want this movement to teach future generations and asked, "Will the lesson be that those in powerful positions ultimately have all the power or that the power of the people is stronger than a flawed system?" I felt inspired and desired to empower every single person in that room. As I finished speaking I was shocked to see people jump to their feet in a standing ovation! Did this mean what I thought it meant? Had people changed their mind about returning? Were we all truly "awake"? Indeed we were. When a vote was taken it was overwhelmingly in favor of staying out with only nine votes to return. I felt encouraged. I felt relieved. I felt scared. Mingo had just gone wildcat. Our ancestors would be proud. ✖

PEIA
STAND with
WV TEACHERS
#FixPEIA
Support State
Employees
HOW CAN YOU
HELP?
CALL Write
E-MAIL THE
AND

Though I hope to never
need to live through
that type of experience
again, I'll never forget
how I felt in that moment:
revolutionary.

—Jacob Staggers

Jacob Staggers
South Morgantown Middle School, Monongalia County

We'd been screwed. It was the only thought I could contemplate as I moped around my apartment on February 28, 2018. For the past week, I'd been living my life on the road between Morgantown, where I work as an English teacher at South Middle School, and Charleston, our state capitol. I proudly wore my homemade strike shirt, and I'd constructed a sign out of foam boards and wooden rods that functioned as a drum that I pounded when I stood in the lobby outside the Senate chambers. I was living off of fast food and coffee. I was tired of waking up at 3:45 a.m. to drive two and a half hours to make sure I made it to the capitol early enough to get inside quickly, and fed up with the lack of concessions we were seeing from the House and Senate Republicans.

However, the night before, I'd felt crushed by the union leaders in whom I'd placed my trust. They'd taken a deal with our governor, a billionaire who flip-flopped parties as soon as he was elected. He'd promised us a 5 percent raise, though our fellow state employees would only see 3 percent. Furthermore, he'd offered a task force to address our insurance concerns sometime in the future, and there was no promise for transparency with that. Even more concerning, none of our legislative concerns, such as seniority being compromised or funding being diverted away from public education, were addressed at all in this deal. The thing that made this moment so frustrating was that we had momentum. We'd shut the entire state education system down multiple days in a row. All fifty-five counties were on board, and we felt strong! The public was even supporting our efforts, for the most part anyways. However, our union leaders had signed all of our progress away in a single meeting with the governor, and I was furious.

After a day of sulking, I decided the inevitable day of school the following morning merited some planning. I decided on what my kids and I would be doing. I laid out some comfortable clothing, and then took a shower. I was planning to go to bed early, since the next morning would be emotional. I dreaded facing my kids, hearing them ask if we'd won our "strike," and having to answer honestly that I didn't feel we'd won anything. It was around 7:10 p.m. when I climbed out of the shower and saw my phone was filled with recent text messages and missed calls. I checked the first few, still in the buff and dripping wet. An emergency, non-union-sanctioned meeting was being held by concerned Monongalia County teachers at the Old Morgantown Mall, a shopping center that is mostly vacant these days except for a few businesses that house their operations there. I texted my coworker, Trevor McIntyre, and we agreed we needed to attend that meeting. The trouble was it started in twenty minutes, and I wasn't dry yet, much less dressed. After furiously rushing to rectify both of those issues, I was still pulling on my shoes and buttoning my pants as I ran outside to hop in Trevor's car. We broke multiple traffic laws as we raced across town. We ran into the mall and through the deserted beige corridors until we found the meeting.

The mood was tense. Some teachers felt we'd received what we'd wanted and should go back on good faith and the advice of our union leadership. Others angrily vowed to remain out the following day. There were plans made to block the bus garage exits in the morning if our superintendent didn't change his mind and cancel school. Similar meetings had occurred in other counties, and many school systems in the state were already closed. Finally, both of our county union presidents arrived. They spoke with our superintendent and found he was willing to support us, but he wanted answers regarding why we wouldn't go back the next day. We managed, in spite of anger and fear running rampant around the meeting, to agree that we wanted an even 5 percent raise for all state employees. There was dissension regarding the insurance issue, but most of us were willing to return to work if there was more transparency for the task force. Finally, we wanted all of that in writing and signed by both the Senate and House, along with formal agreements to no longer pursue the legislation we'd been concerned about during the legislative session.

Out of everything we did during the 2018 West Virgina Teachers Work Stoppage, this evening will always stand out to me as the moment we took radical action. The unions had promised to get the teachers back in the classroom. However, they were wrong. A handshake and good faith ended the 1990 strike, but that would not work this time. We'd seen Mitch Carmichael sneering at us as he scoffed at the proposed deal. Even if our less-than-reliable governor could be counted on to support the deal, we knew the Senate would not follow suit. If we went back at that point, we went back as failures.

In fifty-five counties, whether through meetings like ours or through Facebook, phone calls, and text messages, teachers across the state told not only the state government we wouldn't return to our classrooms, but also our union leadership. The next day, once again, all fifty-five counties were closed, and we would fight on a few more days before we'd achieve victory. As we expected, the Senate fought hard against our deal. If not for our superintendents supporting us in person at the capitol, we'd have still likely failed. However, we chose on that dark, cold Wednesday evening to refuse to follow the unions. We were wildcats hell-bent on seeing this fight through. Though I hope to never need to live through that type of experience again, I'll never forget how I felt in that moment: revolutionary. ✖

And then she asked me a question that shook me. She asked if West Virginia teachers were inspired by other movements in the country—most recently, the movement lead by the students of Marjory Stoneman Douglas High School in Parkland, Florida in response to the senseless and horrific school shooting that claimed the lives of seventeen people.

The West Virginia teacher strike began one week after Parkland. And her question was a jarring reminder of what it means to be a teacher in 2018. What it means is teaching is all encompassing. It means packing backpacks so students have enough to eat when they're not in school. It means time away from your own children to give your energy and attention to the children of others. It means counseling, coaching, and finding the light in every child. It means having class at Panera Bread if you have to. It means loving them. It means you are your work and your work is you. It means laying down your life if you have to.

Karla Hilliard
Spring Mills High School, Berkeley County

The West Virginia teacher strike reminded me of what it means to be a teacher. It reminded me of what my friend Jay Nickerson says of teaching—that it "is a human endeavor." And it reminded me of what Parker Palmer says in *The Courage to Teach*, that "my ability to connect with my students, and to connect them with the subject, depends less on the methods I use than on the degree...I am willing to make [myself] available and vulnerable in the service of learning."

My students make it easy. They are spectacular people. They are mathematicians and musicians and athletes and activists. They are young people with deep curiosities, intellectual agility, and a sensibility I can only describe as "down-ness"—or a willingness to be down for difficult and necessary questions and conversations, for connection and community, for fearless vulnerability with one another and with me.

On day eight of the strike, after days of lobbying, legislative games, empty promises, and pizza—lots and lots of pizza—my students and I had class. The weekend before, my husband and I visited the National Portrait Gallery with some old friends, both of whom are Maryland teachers. As our conversation waxed and waned between metro rides and sandwich shops, my friend Cory said something along the lines of, "If you can't bring the kids to their education, bring the education to the kids." These words and this notion stirred something within me, because learning is not, has never been, confined to our classrooms.

For days I'd watched my colleagues and teachers across the state give our students an education, and that education was different in both kind and degree. Students stood on picket lines, wrote editorials, called lawmakers, organized rallies, and learned, first hand, the power of a collective voice.

We met at Panera Bread. I arrived, ordered, and scoped out the best place for our classroom. I shoved together a few inadvertent tables, dug out my copy of *Hamlet*, and waited to see what would happen next.

As my AP Literature students began trickling in, ordering their own sandwiches and coffees and pastries, the unfamiliar became familiar. We were together. We were having class, like a hauntingly familiar dream, where all the people you know are there but you can't quite make sense of the setting or the scene.

We spent the next hour reading Act Three of *Hamlet*. We "read around the table," not assigning parts, but reading from person to person and looping around, pausing at the ends of scenes to discuss and discover the language and the story—what students noticed, what they found noteworthy, why it was all important. And as my students read and discussed and sipped their coffees and laughed, I wanted to hold onto this moment, a moment when I felt more like a teacher than maybe I ever had before, even in the walls of my own classroom.

When it was time to go, we gathered our things and snapped a few pictures. The kids separated the tables, ruffling papers and books, and squeezed out of the compact space of our makeshift classroom. But they didn't leave. Not for a while anyway.

Before my students walked out into the clear, cool day, we reconvened our class once again, for a few moments more, standing together in an open space near the door. We weren't sure what to do, where to go, or what to expect next. But then we hugged, and class was dismissed.

I took a deep breath and decided to linger a bit longer. I grabbed a table and took out my laptop and figured I should get some work done. I still had essays to grade and deadlines to meet. In the time in between I'd tweeted a few pictures of our class meeting, and the magic speed of social media caught up with me. A *New York Times* reporter messaged me and five minutes later, I was giving an interview instead of grading essays.

We, of course, talked about the strike, its purpose, the picket line, the energy in Charleston.

And then she asked me a question that shook me. She asked if West Virginia teachers were inspired by other movements in the country—most recently, the movement lead by the students of Marjory Stoneman Douglas High School in Parkland, Florida in response to the senseless and horrific school shooting that claimed the lives of seventeen people.

The West Virginia teacher strike began one week after Parkland. And her question was a jarring reminder of what it means to be a teacher in 2018. What it means is teaching is all encompassing. It means packing backpacks so students have enough to eat when they're not in school. It means time away from your own children to give your energy and attention to the children of others. It means counseling, coaching, and finding the light in every child. It means having class at Panera Bread if you have to. It means loving them. It means you are your work and your work is you. It means laying down your life if you have to.

I thought of my students who'd just left, so full of life and promise, and I thought of everything they deserve, of everything they'll achieve, of the ways they'll impact their communities and the world.

This is is a movement not about teacher pay but teacher voice. It is a movement that bears testament to what teachers do—what teachers are prepared to do, the roads they're ready to travel, for their students, for our children. ✖

Julie Abel
Teacher Mountain Ridge Middle School, Berkeley County

During the work stoppage I helped organize sites for Mountain Ridge Middle, Intermediate, and its feeder schools, Gerrardstown Elementary, and Back Creek Valley Elementary. I know many teachers and service personnel at these schools. It's where I work and where my sons go to school. Jude, age eleven, is a fifth grader at Mountain Ridge Intermediate. Max, eight, is a third grader at MRI. My boys attended rallies and emergency food packings, and walked the line with me at the Mountain Ridge campus and Back Creek Valley Elementary. On Friday, February 23, day two of the stoppage, Jude was hugging his teachers, holding signs, getting tons of honks from passing vehicles. He was supporting me. He went to the snack table to peruse the goodies so many generous people had left for us. We had a propane torpedo heater, because it was cold, and our feet were wet. He was standing two feet away from it … wearing synthetic pants. (I can't get him to wear anything else, my son loves to be comfortable.)

Suddenly, his pants ignited. He stopped, screamed, and dropped to the ground. My health teacher, Brandon Wagoner, jumped on top of him and beat the flames out. A stranger, I found out later a Frontier employee, had stopped moments before to offer support and tell us about their impending strike. He quickly cut the pants leg, preventing the fabric from melting to Jude's skin. Our school nurse, Dara Randolph, was also there. They used an emergency kit to work on Jude immediately. I was on the ground holding Jude, assuring him the people taking care of him knew what they were doing and everything would be alright. Jude was remarkably calm. He trusted us.

I know I saw a ring of boots standing around us. I don't remember who was next to me with a hand on my back, but I know we were surrounded by our Mountain Ridge family, my co-workers, friends, and my son's teachers. After a trip to the ER, Jude was bandaged, with a second degree burn the size of my hand on

"Heroes are in our midst. Take a look.
Don't let them leave."

his calf. It could have been so much worse. Heroes are in our midst. Take a look. Don't let them leave. I need to work with people who care about their jobs and my boys. I do. I love my job, my students, and my community. The right people at the right time make ALL the difference. They cannot be replaced.

Jude has mended. He has a "battle scar," a "cool strike story," and a nickname from my co-workers, "Blaze." During the work stoppage, my son became a leader, an activist, a part of the legislative process, a service to his community, and a warrior. I am forever grateful to Brandon, Dara, and a stranger. I am thankful for the Mountain Ridge community. I am a proud mom. I am #55ignited. ✖

EMILY HILLIARD: Why are you out here today?

I'm out here because it's been a long time. It's been a really long time and people have been suffering and not able to meet their own needs, and it's hard to go into a school and try to take care of children and meet all of their needs, especially in this climate. I mean, you wouldn't believe the things that we see in the schools. It's tragic--the conditions that poverty has caused, the drug epidemic, and we have just been going so long without getting a raise that will be a sustainable wage and it's just been going on too long.

EH: You were talking about being excited that UMWA guys were out--could you talk a little bit about that?

Yeah! It was very exciting. Yesterday I wasn't here for the rally but it was really thrilling to see those guys come out! They know how to do it. You know? My mom was an organizer for the AFT, you know, years ago, 70s and the 80s, but people my age really don't know how to do that, you know? And it's very cool to have the people that do know how to have the demonstrations, to fund the demonstrations-- like Bud [UMWA member] was talking about a strike fund if it would go that long-- I mean these are the folks that know how to do it, and we need people to teach us how to be effective.

Jessica Salfia
Spring Mills High School, Berkeley County

O n Tuesday February 27, 2018, union leaders Dale Lee and Christine Campbell announced in a joint statement that a deal had been reached. I felt my stomach lurch and my throat close when I heard we would be accepting a 5 percent pay raise and a temporary freeze for PEIA.

I was confused and surprised by this, and then I was angry.

I had spent the first two days of the strike lobbying in Charleston, telling every legislator who would listen that this was never about money, it was about health care, about respect. We wanted PEIA fixed, not frozen. I spent over an hour and a half with Delegate Espinosa, head of the House Education Committee, talking why PEIA should be the focus of every legislator. The changes to PEIA were breaking folks. And most of us knew that if West Virginia could figure out how to fully fund PEIA that would equate to a pay raise for state employees and solve the problem that was keeping most public employees up at night. I was shocked at the deal. A raise and a freeze? A freeze not a fix?

I gritted my teeth and tried to focus on what we had accomplished. I posted something on Facebook like, "No one's happy, but look what we did…" and went to bed anxious to figure out what our next steps would be.

Wednesday February 28 was supposed to be a cooling off day. I was exhausted and was looking forward to a day to reorient myself and my children to a normal routine. I had driven over five hours to Charleston the week before and spent the first two days of the strike lobbying, long days fighting to get face time with legislators. Monday and Tuesday had been spent in the cold on the picket line alongside Route 11 in Spring Mills. I was tired and so was my family.

I logged into Facebook to see what folks were saying about the deal. The first post on my phone was a livestream of the capitol. The halls were filled with red-clad protesters.

Holy hell, we were still there.

"A freeze is not a fix! Today we talk! Tomorrow we walk!" the red-clad army chanted.

It wasn't over. We had gone rogue.

I watched all day as the crowd grew in the capitol grew. And then, Senate Majority Leader Mitch Carmichael went on Hoppy Kercheval's *Talkline* and announced that he wasn't sure if the bill would pass, took the pay raise off the agenda, and adjourned for the day giving every indication that the pay raise would likely not be a priority.

One by one, the counties started started to close, the map of West Virginia school districts turning red. The red wave crept closer and closer to the Eastern panhandle, but both Berkeley and Jefferson counties had announced that schools would be open on Thursday. Union leaders were issuing conflicting information or were silent. My school was organizing through a Facebook Messenger group chat, and by late evening our chat was filled with indecision.

What should we do?
What if Berkeley doesn't close?
We have to stay United!
But the unions told us to go back to work.
Hell with 'em. I was in this to fix PEIA, and that's not done. I'm not going back.
Guys, I think if our school is open we should go back.
We can't! We have to stay united.

I felt sick. I was one of the organizers of this movement in our school, one of the strongest voices advocating to walk. But I had said from the beginning that I was going to do whatever union leaders told me to do. And our unions had said go back to work. I became indecisive. I didn't want to lead my folks, my friends, down a road that could result in people losing their jobs or even worse their friends.

We watched as county after county closed and turned red.

By 10:30 p.m. nearly the entire state of West Virginia had turned red with school closures—every county but Berkeley and Jefferson, the two Eastern panhandle counties.

In our messenger chat group things had become tense, and it was clear that things had become very real. We began organizing.

They're not going to close.
We have to form lines at the entrances and block the cars.
We have to make them cross our line.
Who can meet me at the bus garage at 3:00? We have to have
lines at the bus garage to stop the busses from
being able to run.
Why do we have to block the entrances?
Because that's a real strike. You shut it down and make them
cross your line or they go home. You stop school
from happening.
Oh Jesus, we're going to see people drive through us aren't we?
Yep.
This is awful.
Yes. It just got real.

I was trying to prepare myself for what was to come. I knew I would have to watch some of my colleagues and friends cross a line that I would not and could not cross. I remembered horror stories of friendships that never recovered from the 1990 strike. I can still hear a mentor of mine saying of the 1990 strike, "I remember every face who crossed and what they were wearing. You don't forget betrayal."

I knew our faculty would probably not recover from this. I tried to answer questions in the group chat and be brave, but I couldn't stop crying. I was ready to stand united. I was ready to fight. But I already feared and mourned the cost for my school and community.

Then, just before 11:00 p.m. Berkeley turned red. We had closed.

A sob of relief erupted out of me. The group chat exploded with joy. No one would have to choose yet. No one would have to hate each other.

But now what? We were officially a wildcat strike. Who was negotiating? It was clear the unions has lost control of the movement. The people were leading and I wasn't sure when and how this was going to end, but of one thing I was certain.

West Virginia would stay united. ✖

I Fight For Your Kids Everyday
Teachers
#United
WV
Will You Do The
Sam For Us?

SUTTON ELEMENTARY SCHOOL TEACHER, BRAXTON COUNTY

EMILY HILLIARD: And why are you here today?

Really just support for all this. I mean initially it was our premiums going up, and I already work a second job to pay for things and then I found out that was basically gonna get cancelled out when they started looking at my second job, so I already work pretty hard to stay above the water and started looking like we were gonna drown, I guess.

CATHY KUNKEL*: How long do you think you'll be out here-- any idea?

If I had to put money on it I'd say till next week sometime. I mean, a solution has been brought up, but they keep pushing it aside--they don't want to talk about it. It seems like if they want us in the classrooms they would at least entertain the idea of talking about it. But they keep pushing it aside. And I also feel like if there was no solution like they keep saying there is, then why do we have all this legislative support that we do have out here with us, so...

CK: What's the solution you're referring to?

The big energy corporations, I mean taxing the oil that's kinda lining their pockets right now. Giving it to the people instead of the corporation.

EH: Anything else you wanna add?

Oh no, just stay strong!

*Cathy Kunkel is a writer who helped Emily with the interviews.

Tega McGuffin Toney
Oak Hill High School, Fayette County

Many believe the West Virginia teachers' strike was like a spontaneous combustion, with anger and frustration exploding in a quick and unpredictable burst of energy. The truth is that the strike was a long time in the making and was anything but spontaneous. It was the result of years of teachers feeling anti-public education sentiment was dictating education policy not only on a local and state level, but on a national level as well. Teachers were increasingly feeling as if they were spectators in shaping education policy, rather than experts to be consulted. It was in this spirit that the teacher strike and the mantra of "55 Strong" was born.

Speaking from a labor and union perspective, I can say that activism was on a steady upswing in West Virginia beginning with the 2014 election. Many anti-worker bills and policies were winding their way through the statehouse and landing as passed legislation. Some of these bills and policies dealt directly with the public education system in the form of public charter schools, elimination of seniority rights, introduction of school vouchers, etc. Teachers who also serve as union activists were instrumental in beating back this harmful legislation that would not help address our staggering, and increasing by the day, teacher vacancies in West Virginia.

In addition to these attacks on public education, teachers were consistently bringing home low pay (ranked forty-eighth in the nation) and suffering from yearly take-backs in PEIA insurance. All of these issues combined and led to educators feeling devalued. It was as if their expertise in their fields did not matter deserving neither fair compensation nor respect. This was a common theme throughout the build-up to the strike. Teachers began to mobilize via a Facebook page, through meetings held by local leaders, and through communication with media outlets.

The meetings served two purposes for me as a union leader: to quickly disseminate information and to get my finger on the pulse of my members and co-workers in my county. I quickly realized that people were angry and frustrated, and that this burst of activism would be unlike any West Virginia has ever seen. They were upset at draconian PEIA proposals that would actually result in a pay cut for many, as well as the lack of a raise and a serious investment in our public schools. They were concerned that the number of teacher vacancies would continue to climb as a result of a prolonged attack on public education. They were concerned that politicians were not looking out for the best interest of the kids in the classroom and the experts standing in the front of those classrooms.

Returning to my classroom after the strike was like coming home. My students were full of questions regarding the work action. Perhaps even more heartwarming was when several students said they admired us for our bravery and for teaching them to stand up for what is right. In this country, teachers are some of the bravest people there are; whether it's displayed through standing in front of a room full of teenagers day in and day out, caring for our kids when it seems others will not, taking a bullet for them, or setting down the red ink pen and picking up a sign and marching to the capitol, teachers are living examples of bravery and self-sacrifice. I've never thought of myself as being "brave" in my profession, but oftentimes kids see things through a different lens. When kids made comments such as those, I smiled and told them that they, too, are brave in so many ways.

The work during the strike was grueling, yet rewarding and satisfying. Local union leaders truly were the glue that held many of the teachers together. We held meetings, let our members vent their frustrations, helped them set up picket lines, and had a strong presence in Charleston. Nevertheless, the grassroots activism that sprang from the rank and file members is what made this movement the success that it was, and also what made the message so powerful for the rest of the nation. Even more intriguing is that this new labor movement is led by white collar professionals who are demanding a better life for all middle class and working class families. "55 Strong" is not just a rallying cry for West Virginia teachers; it is a demand for justice and for respect of working families throughout the nation. ✖

The national media is obsessed with the idea of West Virginia as "Trump country." In countless interviews during and after the strike, I was asked the question, "How could this have happened in a state that voted for Trump?" I was initially puzzled at the question; my state has a rich, militant labor history–

I followed in the footsteps of my grandfather and great-grandfather by taking part in the strike.

Emily Comer
South Charleston High School, Kanawha County

The national media is obsessed with the idea of West Virginia as "Trump country." In countless interviews during and after the strike, I was asked the question, "How could this have happened in a state that voted for *Trump*?" I was initially puzzled at the question; my state has a rich, militant labor history—I followed in the footsteps of my grandfather and great-grandfather by taking part in the strike. Surely reporters had done their research? But more importantly, the years of disillusionment with the status quo that led to Trump's popularity laid the groundwork for the strike itself. The shallow narrative of Appalachians voting against our own self-interest completely fails to grapple with our long history of neglect and exploitation by out-of-state interests and our own political class.

It's true that West Virginia has voted red in the last five presidential elections, and that Republicans swept our state legislature in 2014 for the first time in eighty-two years. Yet it's also true that the number of registered independents in our state has soared; Democrats are changing their voter registration, but not to Republican. When I talk to my friends and colleagues, many express distrust in our political parties and institutions of government. Prior to the strike, many had stopped taking part in the democratic process entirely, refusing to vote.

West Virginians have been left with a sense of desperation and hopelessness that comes from years of broken promises by those in charge. The coal industry has left us high and dry, we have rising poverty, our population is declining, and an opioid crisis is ravaging our communities. Teachers and school service personnel, in particular, have a unique window into these effects of the economy when we step into school every day. We have students experiencing homelessness, living in an under-funded foster care system, and facing hunger. Lack of funding for education and healthcare is just one of many failures of leadership that have led to school employees—and the voters of our state—saying enough is enough.

We have seen enough to know that simply voting for Democrats won't fix our problems. Prior to 2016, the so-called party of working people held power in our state for decades and failed to deliver. Throughout their eighty-two years of legislative control, the Democratic Party never granted collective bargaining rights to public employees. In 2007, under Governor Joe Manchin's Democratic leadership, our state government lowered the corporate net income tax from 9 percent to 6.5 percent and began phasing out the business franchise tax entirely, leaving a budget hole of more than $200 million annually. Rather than investing in our schools, public employees, or any number of measures that would help the people of our state, Democrats chose to give millions of dollars in handouts to corporations. These tax breaks were supposed to bring in jobs, but we're still waiting.

Teachers and school employees have been organizing around our healthcare benefits for years because of this bipartisan manufactured emergency, but it's only grown worse. Year after year, we voted, we showed up to hearings, we lobbied, and we asked nicely. This year, we finally decided we were tired of going through the proper channels only to reach a dead end. Our desperation turned into determination, and we took matters into our own hands by leading a historic nine-day statewide strike. The solidarity that made this strike possible was not built along party lines; we were united around a set of shared grievances and people came together with little concern for party affiliation. We had a common goal: to win a material gains that we deserved, to make our lives better as workers.

This unity happened so naturally in the lead-up to the strike that it took some time for me to make sense of the question. *"How did this happen in Trump country?"* It didn't happen in Trump country, it happened in West Virginia, and of course it did. Many well-meaning liberal and progressive folks around the country are so focused on party politics that they lose sight of real people and what's actually important to us. Petty partisan bickering

about Donald Trump's tweets and weekly cabinet rotations played *zero* role in this fight. People cannot afford healthcare—that's do or die. If these same observers are paying attention, they'll note that, save for a handful, Democrats nationwide aren't fighting for healthcare either. Healthcare inflation is a national crisis that won't truly be fixed until we have a universal system like Medicare for All and politicians who are willing to take on the entrenched power of pharmaceutical and insurance companies.

Critically, Democrats in our state legislature sided with public employees during our fight for a raise and healthcare funding this year, but they didn't come to our rescue. We exerted pressure and they responded quickly. Republicans stood in staunch opposition against us until the bitter end. There's no doubt the voters of West Virginia will remember who stood for us and who stood against us come November. However, if workers had not led the charge, we may have never heard a sound from Democratic lawmakers about the need for these measures. If working people are going to keep winning, we can't wait on politicians to save us. We must lead the fight and take our demands straight to those in power. ✖

Knowledge is a
civil right. The first
ingredient to a failed
state is the denial of
learning and the freedom
to create original ideas
from knowledge.

—Daniel Summers

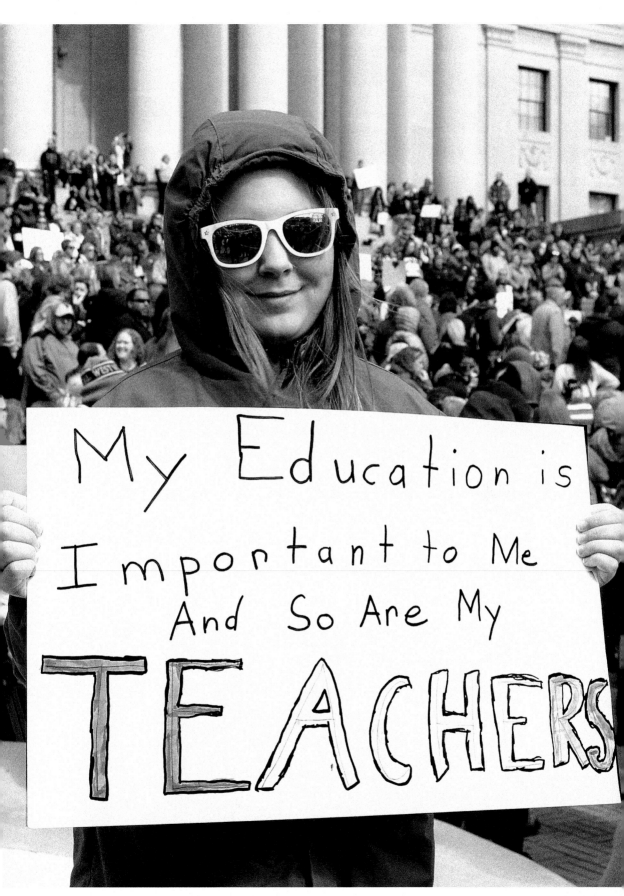

Daniel Summers
University High School, Monongalia County

Five o'clock in the morning is an empty time in a school. The halls, red and old-gold, are waiting for the tenacious brand of learning that is unique to high school. I have to feel my way by the cafeteria. John hasn't turned on all of the lights, or unlocked the cafeteria doors yet. I cut through the computer lab instead.

It is Thursday. A day for wrapping things up and allowing myself to be a little tired, a little contemplative. Usually by Thursday, I am drained and waiting for coffee to convert itself to strength.

Today, I have plenty of strength. It seeps into me. I feel like a giant; I know how mighty teachers can be.

We haven't acquired much—but we stood—we refused to let closed minds take integrity and livelihood from West Virginia's public employees—from education. Our mantra, "55 Strong," wasn't a battle cry or a slogan. It wasn't union propaganda or a glittering generality. It was a truth. We were strong. We left the picket line, but our legislators need to know: we are still strong.

From where we stood, it was the determination of educators against the stubbornness of broken legislators and greed. At the risk of showing my ego, testing the determination of teachers is a folly.

Now, I am back. I have a sign propped against my white board. It is battered and broken. It says: "Today I teach perseverance." It is the sign I held every day of the teacher work stoppage. It still has a muddy footprint in the bottom left corner. Likely from some negligent dancing on the line.

When we do vocabulary in my class, I often make students close their eyes and envision the connotative meaning of a word. I stress that language's power comes from what is inside us, not from what is written in a dictionary.

A student asked me, "Mr. Summers, what is the connotative meaning of perseverance?" I told her that it is the line between who I am right now and who I want to be tomorrow. It is the line between the world I live in and the world I want to help shape. She asked me if it worked.

It will if I don't stop—that is what I believe. I told her I may never find out.

I used to memorize poetry, so that when I ran I had something to recite in my head. I tried out different rhythms with each footfall. When I became a teacher I stopped. Now I memorize aha moments in my classroom. I remember reading Mary Oliver's "Wild Geese" and a student crying because he had been convinced that people weren't allowed to make mistakes and still be good. I remember the quiet girl from the back of the room who shook the whole time she presented, but refused to sit down. "I need to know I can do this," she said.

I have spent the last four years, as a teacher, living paycheck to paycheck. In Monongalia County, I am fortunate to be one of the highest-paid starting teachers in the state of West Virginia. And yet, I have almost no money left over once the essentials are covered. Even with the $2,020 raise, I will still be in an uphill battle financially. My insurance is my biggest fear. I have two children and affordable, solid insurance is a priority for their well being. This is a story that many Americans can relate to. Teachers do not have a monopoly on being underpaid and unjustly insured.

But, we stood. We stood because labor is underappreciated. We stood because the potential of a mind is valued less than the money that can be gained from non-progressive, partisan policies. We stood because public employees are the foundation of an upward-moving society. In this state that foundation is crumbling. Without good educators, state troopers, and other public servants we lose essential security and rights. Knowledge is a civil right. The first ingredient to a failed state is the denial of learning and the freedom to create original ideas from knowledge.

I am a collector of the things my students synthesize. I see knowledge go into them and come back out as measurable ideas. Great teachers collect these moments and keep them to be recreated again and again among a diverse population of students. I have fallen in love with potential. I think most of us stood because, at its core, a refusal to make West Virginia a haven for educators is a roadblock to our students' right to highly qualified knowledge.

Certainly, I would like to make more money. That isn't why I walked out; the raise is not why I came back. I walked because I believe West Virginia is better than the current leaders who support outside industries before our foundation and infrastructure, and before our educators and other public workers. I will persevere so West Virginia today has a chance to grow better tomorrow. I came back because our legislatures and governor agreed to compromise and discuss our needs civilly.

Really, we walked because we were strong, and we came back because we are still strong. Unity and solidarity build strength. West Virginians understand that. It is woven into our sense of place. We do not want anything; we are screaming that there are needs. The core of this state—its best resource—are the people who stay here and use their minds and bodies to better the region. That core, that resource is bleeding. The work stoppage did not stop or slow the bleeding, but it did point out the wound. We handed Congress a needle and thread. But, we are strong enough to stand again, if they decide to apply another Band-Aid.

The school is quiet at five o'clock in the morning. It is tense with an approach of angst, joy, and all things high school. Aha moments are near. Giants wait for students to stand on their shoulders. I wish that everyone could stand for a moment on this end of learning. See the wave of students swim through the halls like salmon. Upstream they fight every day, instinctually trying to reach their potential; only faintly aware of what that is. It is my job to make sure they make it through this stage of the journey with a little more strength. If I keep some memories, well that is my real pay. I hope enough people see how worth it this feeling is. I hope that we fight to keep qualified individuals in the public sector. West Virginia deserves it. ✖

Elizabeth Catte

CONCL

We all remember our favorite teachers. We tuck their small acts of kindness away in basements or in attic boxes: red-penned lines of encouragement, our worth acknowledged. We remember their handwriting and the wooden, waxy smell of their classrooms. Many of us continue to do good work in their names, and this is especially true of individuals who later became teachers themselves.

I am honored to be part of your introduction to some of our favorite teachers. When you put this book back on your shelf or pass it along to a friend, I hope you will remember them and how much they mean to us. The education strikes sweeping the nation are part of a large and unstoppable movement, but movements are made of people who animate our struggles and personify what it means to take action. This glimpse inside one movement has brought you people like Erin Marks, who collected donations for food banks during the strike, and Brandon Wolford, who kept the memories of his father and grandfather walking the line close when it was his turn.

USION

The joyful and candid photographs of the strike, taken by Emily Hilliard, are an important record of this moment, but it is also important to reflect on what cameras didn't see. The strike looked like hundreds of teachers filling the capitol, with Parry Casto chanting them hoarse, but it also looked like Karla Hilliard reading *Hamlet* with her students at a coffee shop and Mark Salfia sending that daily e-mail to his colleagues to remind them they were strong. It looked like Jacob Staggars running red lights to get across town in time to vote for the wildcat strike, and Julie Abel packing meals with her children so that students who relied on their schools for breakfasts and lunches would still be able to have those during the strike.

Tega McGuffin Toney, a union leader, and Jay O'Neal, a grassroots organizer, described the slow burn of unrest that ignited in February. That action came to us through the movement of workers in unison but also through so many moments, alone in cars or at kitchen tables, fretting over bills and benefits. Before there were battered signs and chants, there were clipboards, text messages, and public hearings. The question, "Should we strike?" translated to many others, heard and unheard: "What happens if I get sick?" "How can students succeed without skilled teachers?" "What can I do without this month?"

The call to strike resonated deeply in southern West Virginia where the rich legacy of labor organizing is personal. The past was there, in the sharp and cold mornings, when the teachers of the coalfields rose to take their place in a long tradition. "The willingness to stand is part of our DNA," Katie Endicott writes. What did southern teachers fear? Not repercussions from an illegal strike, not failure: their dread came from the thought that refusing to take action would betray the living memories of their ancestors. When Robin Ellis, from Mingo County, had to teach herself how to sustain a strike, she relied on classroom pedagogy—she identified the strike's rising actions and turning points, much like a student reading a novel—and her husband, a retired United Mine Workers of America member. Even coalfield students like Isabella Grace can tell you, almost effortlessly, what solidarity means. The descendants of the Mine Wars have inherited the Mind Wars. March on.

To enhance that connection, we've inserted small callbacks in this volume that make the past burn brighter. These callbacks—illustrations, font choices, images—aren't just visual accessories but a portal to this moment and how workers described, here and in other interviews, what the strike felt like for them. When they reached for the alarm clock at 5:00 a.m., they thought of their parents and grandparents who worked in the mines and agitated for the dignity of their labor. When they laid on their car horns passing a picket line, they imagined their mothers and grandmothers doing the same during the 1990 teachers' strike. "His hand was callused and strong. It felt like my Papaw's hand," Jessica Salfia writes of greeting a union member who joined them on the line. What we wouldn't give, some of us, to hold the people who inspire us close again. But we remember.

In corners of classrooms are signs and artifacts from the strike, reminders of the unbreakable bond between teachers and their students. Daniel Summers's sign reads: "Today I teach perseverance." What is perseverance? The space between the world we live in now and the world our actions are helping to re-shape. One of his students' favorite poems is Mary Oliver's "Wild Geese":

"The world offers itself to your imagination, calls to you like the wild geese, harsh and exciting—over and over announcing your place in the family of things."

What was the breaking point? For many teachers, it was the idea that without education, without students trained by skilled teachers, there would be no future for West Virginia, no family of things for young people to stake their claim to. A corporation does not love a place; it does not go to weddings and funerals and baby showers. A pipeline or a gas hub won't write your children a letter of recommendation or arrive at a school before daybreak to prepare and serve their meals. A tax break doesn't coach sports or proofread a job application. And we have decades of proof that courting business does not translate into investment in education, only the opposite.

Re-shaping our world requires clear eyes as well as determination. As Emily Comer describes in her essay, the rank-and-file of West Virginia know what it is like to be bereft of powerful allies, and their betrayal cuts across the political spectrum. As much as the strike calls to us to make a blueprint of how this moment came to be, it also calls to us to be the architects who build something different. In Appalachia, we have never been witness to a time when people were as valuable as our extractable resources but our potential to transform this complicated place has never been greater. Because teachers and education workers stood together, and are still standing together in solidarity with workers across the country, we remember that our most powerful allies are one another.

I spent two days in West Virginia during the strike, overwhelmed and filled with love. We drove aimlessly, finding picket lines on almost every corner and blessing each traffic light that allowed us more time to wave and shout support. West Virginia University invited me to speak at an event in Morgantown and what a gift it was to share space with people electrified by their history, each of us imagining our connections to people in the past who marched, walked the line, felt the cold, and still pushed on. No one needed to ask what their place might be in this new movement. A reckoning had been called, and the people were assembled.

The book that you are holding is a brief record of those moments and how they felt to the people who experienced them. We want you to better understand the mechanics of the strike and the issues that compelled it, but we are unapologetically insistent that the most important thing you take from us is how good it felt to be #55STRONG. Other emotions populate the stories—fear, fatigue, anger, relief—but what unites each narrative, across geography and role, is the righteous joy of finding purpose and seeking justice. This is the lesson, these are the tools.

Such stories are a rare commodity in our present moment, and rarer still in places like West Virginia, where it feels like canon that each dispatch must, like thumbs dug into a bruise, make reference to complacency. No one knows the consequences of that canon better than teachers like Jessica, who worked tirelessly during the strike not only to lobby for specific gains but to upend the narrative about education to center what students and teachers deserve. "I knew from the beginning of this movement that our success would hinge on our ability to elevate teacher voices, to tell our stories," she writes.

We agree, and we are grateful to Jessica for letting us do our part to elevate those voices and connecting us to teachers who were eager to share their stories. The speed with which this volume came together, and the enthusiasm among contributors for the project, is a testament to how important it is to make room for people to narrate their own experiences. As the momentum for education strikes continues to build across the country, we hope that teachers in other states know that we are in solidarity and look forward to hearing their voices and seeing their images however they come.

You are part of this, too. You might not work in education, or you might live far from West Virginia, but you are one of us. If you are a person who deserves better, you are one of us. If you love someone who deserves better, you are one of us. If you can't be silent, you are one of us. How could you not be? Take your place. ✖

Acknowledgements

Thank you to the folks at Belt for wanting to tell the story of the incredible educators who organized and led a movement in West Virginia and who have inspired so many other teachers across the country to start their own movements. Thank you to the bus drivers, service personnel, aides, cooks, and public employees who stood in solidarity with West Virginia teachers and kept us 55 United. The success of the West Virginia Work Stoppage would not have been possible without service personnel. Thank you to all the students who stood beside us on the picket line in the cold and the rain, holding signs and showing support. Thank you to the Berkeley County community for the seemingly never-ending supply of food, hot coffee, and love. Thank you to my grandfather, my Aunt Fran, my Uncle Danny, and my mom for showing me what courage looks like. Thank you to my husband, Mark, for cheering every time I get out my laptop, and for being a brilliant educator and leader. And finally, thank you to the brave teachers of Spring Mills High who stood shoulder to shoulder for almost two weeks along an intersection on Route 11 and gave me the courage and the strength to keep going: Craig, Chris, Andrew, Mallory, Brettney, Vikki, Jenny, Ryan, Sarah, Brittny, Shelby, Priscilla, Lisa, Kathy, Annette, Jana, Tonya, Andrew, Ben, Liz, Moira, Tina, Jeanne, Karla, Ed, Tom, Taylor, Wendy, Angela, Lee, Kim, Misty, Matt, Jessica, Hannah, Corey, and Rose. — *Jessica Salfia*

About the Editors

Elizabeth Catte is a historian and writer based in Virginia's Shenandoah Valley. She is the author of *What You Are Getting Wrong About Appalachia* and her work has also appeared in *Belt Magazine*, the *Guardian*, the *Nation*, and *Salon*. She holds a PhD in public history and is the co-owner of Passel historical consultants.

Emily Hilliard is a West Virginia-based folklorist and writer. She holds an M.A. in folklore from the University of North Carolina and is a 2018 recipient of the Parsons Fund Award from the American Folklife Center at the Library of Congress. Her work has been published by *The Bitter Southerner*, *Ecotone*, NPR, *Southern Cultures*, and *West Virginia University Press*, among others.

Jessica Salfia is teacher, writer, and activist. She currently teaches English and Creative Writing at Spring Mills High School in Martinsburg, West Virginia. In 2015 she received an Arch Coal Teaching Award, she was named Berkeley County Teacher of the Year in 2016, and in 2018 she was awarded a Stephen L. Fisher Excellence in Teaching Award from the Appalachian Studies Association Conference. Her writinag has appeared in the *Anthology of Appalachian Writers*, volumes III, V, VI, VII, VIII, IX, and X, the *Charleston-Gazette Mail*, *Belt Magazine*, and the West Virginia Council of Teachers of English Best Practices Blog. She is the co-director of the West Virginia Council of Teachers of English and has been a West Virginia public educator for over 15 years.